Ar~~~~
Pudding
is
Possible

by
Tom Wallace

Other books by Tom Wallace:

Conatus

Twenty-One Levels of Self-Deception

Three Miles of Rice Pudding

Utopia Governance and the Commons

A Little Book about Climate Change

Wild Body Wild Nature

Tales from a Distant Shore

Dreamtree

Table of Contents

Preface

The way to Utopia may not be what you expect!
The story of Cockaigne, a medieval version of
utopia, is much like many other versions of
utopia. It is always Spring, there is perfect
weather, a fountain of youth and abundant food.
The residents of Cockaigne are paid to sleep.
No-one ventures to ask where all the food
comes from or other such technical questions.
The unique thing about Cockaigne though is how
it is reached. You see, access to Cockaigne
requires would-be utopians to eat their way
through three miles of rice pudding. It seems
that the rice pudding journey is an ordeal to be
endured rather than a first taste of pleasures to
come. Learning of this, I wondered if those
journeying to Cockaigne open tunnels in the
pudding through which others might follow. Or
does the pudding simply close up behind them
as they journey through? If so, how do they
breathe, or even see their way to the next meal
of pudding that would bring them closer to their
goal? The perils of the journey seem to be
numerous, even for those who, like me, have a
particular fondness for rice pudding. But the
prize is great! So I invite you to take up your
spoon with me and plunge in. We have three
miles to travel. Whatever your taste in
puddings, it's going to be a sticky journey. But,
I suggest, we need our visions of utopia so that
we might face the future. Let us eat pudding
together!
The stories in this book were first published
individually via the websites Booksie.com and
Storywrite.com. They are based on memoirs
recorded in an earlier work, *Three Miles of Rice
Pudding.*

Another Pudding is Possible

Another Pudding is Possible

A tale where the author finally gets the message that his father doesn't like rice pudding!

It started with a little group of artists in the small city of Dundee, on the East coast of Scotland. I was living with my Dad as his carer at the time. We were in our home town of Newport-on-Tay, which faces Dundee across the mouth of the River Tay.

The artists had started a monthly silent walk on a Saturday in Newport and I decided to join them. After one of the walks we are gathered at the home of two of the artists who also lived in Newport.

At the artists' house, someone has a guitar. There are a lot of postcards in the house where we have gathered. The guitarist and I set about making up songs – telling stories about what the postcards might be depicting. It is a happy time – someone even scribbles down the lyrics as we weave our songs.

As I said, I was living with my Dad as his carer at the time. The menu for my meals with Dad was fairly consistent – both of us being creatures of habit. Saturday dinner's dessert course was always a rice pudding. Back at Dad's house, the rice pudding is in the oven. Eventually, fear for its fate overcomes the desire to stay on at the artists' house and continue with the song-making. I rush home. I catch the pudding just in time.

I had lived with my Dad for about three years by then and every Saturday delivered a rice pudding as the crowning glory of the week's menu. However, it was on that very Saturday of the silent walk and the singing and story-telling that my Dad explained he did not in fact like rice pudding. Communication had never been our strong point. I was reminded of the ancient stories of a utopia called Cockaigne. Strangely, access to Cockaigne could only be achieved by eating through three miles of rice pudding. I had subjected my father to – if not three miles of rice pudding – then certainly three years of weekly doses. Laid end to end, and with a seven-inch bowl, it comes to around thirty-five yards. It would have taken another 171 years of weekly puddings for my Dad to traverse the three miles to the mythical utopia of Cockaigne, and he was already 92.

But I like to think that I am not a hard-hearted son. Rice pudding was replaced by trifle from then on. Another world might not be possible, but for my Dad at least, another pudding was possible. In truth though, Saturdays were never quite the same.

Caring for an elderly relative is a strange experience. In my mind it has become linked to our human obsession with utopia – both personal utopias and utopias designed for whole societies. I know that probably sounds a bit obscure, so let me explain.

First there is that time in our lives (if our parents live long enough) when you, the child, start to be seen as the 'responsible adult'. It might be at a restaurant, when the waitress automatically places the bill in front of you rather than your father or mother. Or it might be during some medical consultation about one of your parents, where the doctor addresses all of their comments to you rather than your Mum or Dad, even although the consultation is about them.

Such events set off a trail of thoughts in my head. Dad's life was once in the ascendant. He had hopes and dreams about building a future for himself, through study and work. Then he met Mum and together they planned to find a house, to make that house a home and to make it a safe and loving home for the family they had together. A personal utopia therefore. Perhaps not perfection, but as good as my parents could make it.

Society in general has similar aims. Opportunities for study. Meaningful work. Improving lifestyles. Safety. Home. Human flourishing. There comes a point, like those moments in our personal lives, when we realise that whether society is good or bad is down to us – we are the responsible adults.

But then the inevitable decline as illness, old age and frailty set in. How does Dad or Mum feel about this? It's a difficult thing to witness – a difficult thing to discuss. The child can only

9

hope that their parents don't feel that their efforts to build a life for themselves have been in vain. In short, you hope that you've not been a disappointment to them! You hope that they are proud of their offspring!

Time, then, is what makes the difference in a human life – from starting out with hope and optimism to our last days – looking back with either satisfaction or disappointment, or a mixture of the two.

And time is likewise a factor for society. To think of an ideal way for humans to live together in peace and prosperity is difficult enough. That is like our youthful aspiration – and often the aspect of utopia that people think of as naïve. But to make a society that is resilient in the long-term – through changes in culture, changes in economic conditions, changing environmental conditions, changing international relations – well, that's another thing altogether.

Society, of course, does not face an inevitable decline of old age and death. There are always new generations of people coming up to replace those who are lost. But still there is a particular kind of care needed for both individuals and human societies in general. Indeed care for the elderly and for everyone else has a special place in society at large. It is that aspect of society that is so often hidden and so often provided for free. Without care the world of consumer capitalism would collapse!

For our parents, and other folk we may know, we need to remember that great legacy in their lives – those hopes and dreams of their youth. For society, can we likewise cherish all those dreams of utopian futures that we all share when we reflect on the state of the world?

And for both the elderly person and the mature

society we can say there is the task of ensuring that their lives have not been lived in vain – that we are proud sons and daughters and also proud citizens.

To abandon these things is to shut off all possibilities – both individually and culturally. It is to say life is not worthwhile. The glass is half-empty. There is no point in trying. Things will never change.

I hope things will not be this way. I hope we can always say there is hope! Another pudding is possible! Another world is possible!

Another Pudding is Possible

Chocolate, Alcohol and Skimpy Swimwear

A tale where snacking and swimwear may prove a distraction...

As I mentioned I had joined an arts group in Dundee. It had the clever name of Dundee Artists in Residence – the acronym working out to D-AiR. We're artists – we can do anything – is a phrase I often use. Daring to do stuff is part of the deal – daring to be ourselves – daring to do stuff others won't try – daring to say things others won't say.

The arts group had arranged a swim in the River Tay at Broughty Ferry, a posh suburb of Dundee. We were hosted by 'Ye Ancient Amphibians Society' and met at the harbour. There is a little building there with toilets and small changing rooms. It was June, but as each of us emerged ready to take to the water, we displayed multiple layers of swimwear and wetsuits. All that is except Doug. A cheer went up as he strode out in just a tiny pair of pink Speedos. Someone had a camera and we gathered for a group photo. Doug was at the front, striking a series of body-building poses.

The tide was low, so it meant a long climb down a metal ladder bolted to the side of the harbour wall. But at last, in the water, we just bobbed around and chatted. I spotted someone I knew and swam over to her. She had so many layers of wetsuit it was like she had become an inflatable dinghy.

A proper sandy beach starts from Broughty Ferry and continues North and East for many miles on the North side of the Tay Estuary. After our swim we headed there. Sand was blowing in a stiff breeze, but someone had brought a tent. I gratefully clambered inside, along with four or five others. It's a bit of a squash, but luckily I had some resources in the form of a flask of hot chocolate and a large bar of fruit and nut. I explained to the others that fruit and nut chocolate counts towards one's five a day. I shared out the goodies and everyone seems contented.

Outside, meanwhile, more hardy souls had built a bonfire. As the sun went down and the wind dropped, we all enjoyed some simple food and drinks around the fire.

Days such as these are memorable days. Nothing much happens perhaps but nonetheless there is a lot of satisfaction in time spent with friends, food, drink and some fun activities. Many utopias of the past took this theme – simple pleasures. It's a good idea for a utopia, provided we don't stop to ask where the food and drink comes from, who makes the clothes and the tents, how did we light the bonfire, and so on. The other thing to notice is the general benevolence of people. Perhaps the theory goes – given enough food, drink and entertainment and people won't have any reason to fight each other. It's a very optimistic view of human nature!

Some modern utopias still play on these themes. There's a bright future, it is claimed, that can be brought about by technology. Other utopias hark back to a lost Arcadia (an Arcadia that never really existed). This is a world of small villages, simple agriculture and none but the most basic technologies. Sometimes such simple worlds are offered as a response to climate change.

Whether you consider any such utopias to be desirable, they all face a couple of challenges if they were ever to be put into practice. The first thing is that the world is always changing, so any utopia offered to us must be able to accommodate changing circumstances. The other thing to say is that we humans take a bit of organising! As I've said, the benevolence of people, and indeed good relationships at all levels of society, are things that many utopian stories either assume or ignore. But this seems critical. We are political animals, so there needs to be some effective system of governance to go along with all the promises of the bright future a utopia might offer. The governance system in fact is going to be the thing that addresses the issue of change that I mentioned earlier. So we might say that a large part of resilience comes from good governance.

What might a utopian governance system be like? I can only say that there are a few basic things that we seek as humans. Amongst these are fairness, equality, freedom and justice. And to be genuinely utopian we should add the opportunity for human flourishing in the mix – the opportunity for each person to reach their full potential. This is a bit like the 'dare' in our artists' group with which I started – to be able to be ourselves, speak our minds and express our gifts and talents as people is a big part of human flourishing. I admit though that these are all rather abstract aims. There needs to be some very pragmatic decisions made by a society in order to balance out the idealism of a utopian vision with its mission of achieving fairness, equality, freedom, justice and flourishing.

What if all this could be achieved? Then, at last, we could settle back into those happy days of friends and family, recreation, food and drink, shared conversations, art, music, literature – in short, all the things, both simple and profound, that raise our lives above the level of mere survival. It's a strange feature of utopias that they often bring together the deeply personal – body, food, family, friends, pleasure – with the really big questions of politics and economics.

Should we dare then to dream? Utopian dreams are often despised these days. But if we are not aiming for utopia then what exactly is it that society and culture are aiming at? A reasonable level of mediocrity? A chance to do our own thing as individuals? Efficiency? Safety? These seem like lesser dreams to me and unworthy of us. Let's dream big again! Let's dream of utopia!

I Own my Skin, I Own These Clothes and I Own This Little Patch of Ground!

A tale where torn up currency leads to reflections on ownership and property.

Whilst staying near the small Scottish city of Dundee I had, you may remember, joined a group of artists called D-AiR (Dundee Artists in Residence). We had fun with this acronym being so close to 'dare' and dared many experiments in art along the way. The group had sort of morphed into a new group – the Dundee Commons – with many of the artists crossing over to join the new group. To give it its official title, we were 'If the city were a commons' – so very much about ideas around ownership, sharing and community.
Our first meeting is in a little café that forms

part of a large church and associated halls. Quite a lot of folk have shown up and I am distracted looking around at the people as the meeting gets under way. So I have not really taken in the introductory blurb and before I know it our host for the evening divides us into pairs. Then he picks up some five-pound notes (this was back in the day when fivers were still paper). He tears each note into two halves and presents the halved notes to each of the pairs. There seems to be no explanation, or perhaps I have missed the explanation. Thoughts of sellotape come to mind. My partner and I could simply re-connect our two halves of the note and spend the money on something useful, like chocolate or alcohol. Maybe though, our shared wealth should be used for some 'higher' purpose? Should we give the money to a beggar? Perhaps we should keep the money and see how things unfold with the Commons project? Perhaps the meaning of the split notes would be made clear in future weeks. My partner is not big on conversation, so we kind of fall into that final alternative as the default option.

My five-pound partner did not return to the Commons Group, so our note never did get joined. My half languished on a shelf at home until plastic notes replaced paper ones, and its faint promise of wealth was finally extinguished.

Part of the five-pound note message was of course to question the meaning of ownership. And ownership, let's face it, is a peculiar concept. I might claim, for instance, to own my own body. It's not an unreasonable claim! But could we say that a tree or a plant 'owned' itself in the same way? Perhaps yes, perhaps not. How about a stem cell, or a virus? There comes a point on the evolutionary tree where the concept of owning ourselves loses its meaning! We need, it seems, to have a certain level of agency and consciousness before the idea of owning ourselves means anything.

We could think of clothes as the next most immediate and personal instance of ownership. But we might briefly mention the world of tattoos, body piercings, jewellery and the like that forms a strange hinterland half way between bodies and artefacts. Humans are unique in this – unless we count the weird things people do with their pet dogs! We make things very immediately part of ourselves when it is a mark on the skin or a piercing or incision that is difficult or impossible to remove. But we also say something to the world by the way that we decorate our bodies. This is the cross-over these things have with clothes – they are all statements.

This is perhaps something of a digression, this visit to tattoos and piercings, but I mention it because it shows that the notions of ownership and property are slippery and strange.

The statements we make with our clothes may be about our wealth, our status, our class, our gender – any number of things. Function plays only a small part in the story. It is culture that provides us with the social clues that give meaning to all this. The messages are often powerful – this is much more than just who can afford more durable or warmer clothes.

So clothes and the various items we carry around with us are statements of identity. Who we are as people – or who we like to think we are – is expressed through clothing. This is why uniforms can be a bit disturbing. The uniform denies a person their unique identity.

Sometimes this is reassuring. The policeman, nurse or judge sets aside their personal self for a while and represents the state. And hopefully the state is doing its job of looking after us! But sometimes of course the actions of the state can feel threatening. And then the uniforms worn by its representatives become sinister. States that wish to promote some kind of equality amongst their citizens (as if that is going to be possible) try extending the use of uniforms to everyone. It is, to say the least, a very superficial way of promoting equality! We are more complex creatures than this!

So what about that ultimate claim of ownership – owning a piece of ground? Earlier we noted that it is a kind of natural thing for conscious beings with agency to claim ownership of their bodies. Could we say the same for the Earth herself? That might be a bit of a stretch! But generally, it has to be said, the idea of some person (or animal, bird, or plant) 'owning' a bit of the Earth is equally puzzling. As a child I was concerned with the idea of a piece of land continuing downwards, as a very long pyramid, to the centre of the Earth. Here, everyone's piece of ground meets at a point. But it's more puzzling above ground! Every land owner has an ever-expanding slice of sky, which, depending on the large-scale structure of the universe, would eventually reach the edge of space, or continue forever and therefore be infinitely big, or would somehow curve back on itself. Things get even more complex when you think about owners of land on the moon or other planets, whose slices of space would then intersect with Earth-bound owners! And what if you live in a flat? (Suffice to say, I was an unusual child.)

Perhaps a more pragmatic concern over land ownership however is that benefit accrues to the land owner that very often deny benefits to those who are not owners. This is a particularly entrenched and insidious consequence of land – so much so that it is almost a golden rule of economics! Apart from the unfairness involved, it can also lead to destruction. The peculiarities of land ownership are often at the root of pollution, loss of bio-diversity, and the odd (and usually negative) impacts on the design of towns and cities.

Sharing land – holding land as a commons – is then such an obvious benefit when you think about it in terms of fairness, protection of the environment and enhancing our urban spaces. Those split five-pound notes, with which we started this story, are telling us about the need for co-operation. Money is meaningless without a society to ascribe value to it. And it could also be said that money is useless unless there is a background of co-operation to make the money work for the benefit of society.

We spent some time thinking about owning our bodies and our clothes and the various gadgets we have around us and we saw how important these are to our sense of identity and status.

There is something wonderful about the quirkiness of how we decorate our bodies and the weird world of fashion. Our sense of ownership of course extends itself into the notion of real estate. Here we find oddities, obsessions and fanaticism that once again demonstrate the peculiar ways we approach questions of ownership and property. When it comes to real estate, the quirkiness of human nature can be for both good and ill. I'd suggest the challenge is to find some way to retain the good and avoid the ill.

The straight up kind of solution, in order to avoid the many pitfalls I've mentioned above, is to think of ourselves as custodians of land and real estate. We need to see it as a shared resource even when we own it outright. We need to see it as a commons. And a commons is not an easy thing. It takes work and commitment to achieve and sustain it. And before all that, there's the task of convincing people it's even a thing worth having.

In a memorable phrase, British journalist and author George Monbiot has advocated 'private sufficiency, public luxury', and this very neatly captures the benefits we might gain if we could only get our heads around this land ownership and commons conundrum. But well, at this point I cannot help thinking of my own local council's efforts towards 'public good'. It feels like we are not so subtly being lured into a care home, where the chairs are plastic and the walls are painted hearing-aid beige. That's why I've stressed all the quirkiness in our behaviours around ownership and property above. Somehow, I think, if we were to make 'public luxury' work, we would have to capture that strange spirit that currently manifests in private eccentricities! The straight up solution of just changing the politics around land use is not going to captivate or inspire us.

I think we could have flourishing and pollution-free eco-systems, bountiful nature, beautiful cities and thriving communities if we were willing to think our way around the peculiarities of ownership with which we are currently fixated and, I'd hazard, think outside the box. Could we find a way of joining up our five-pound notes to do something both inspiring and amazing?

Could we capture private eccentricity in public space? I think that would be a change worth trying for.

Another Pudding is Possible

Tragedies, Hot Dogs and Flourishing

In which the author narrowly misses the opportunity for new underwear and where academic disputes are settled by means of hot dogs.

As I've mentioned, in the small city of Dundee, on the East coast of Scotland, I'm part of a group of artists who have embarked on a project called 'If the city were a commons'. We learn there is a bit of money available to fund the year-long project. We're all going to be putting in some effort to the project – so should we divvy up this money? There are about twenty of us at this stage, so it doesn't work out to much. Why bother? – that's my feeling, as the conversation is drifting on. Then my thoughts start to turn to what a commons should really be doing with money – and indeed stuff generally. I imagine us all getting into the hall next to the café where we are meeting. We have brought our belongings in suitcases, boxes and wheelbarrows. It is all deposited in a large heap on the floor. The lights are switched off. We all undress and add our clothes to the pile of stuff. Then it's open season, to rummage through the loot and get kitted out with new clothes, books and whatever else takes our fancy. Now that would be a commons!

That view – that a commons is about divvying things up on an equal basis – is, I must confess, a bit misleading. A commons can certainly be about shared resources. Often it is land, but it might also be a forest, a fishing ground or even buildings and artefacts. Recently the term commons has been associated with even broader things. The atmosphere, for instance, may be a commons, and the oceans and even the solar system. This might be a useful way of expanding our environmental awareness. But I have to say that to be of practical use the idea of a commons needs to be local and it needs to be about close co-operation within a small community.

Anyone who has heard of 'the commons' has usually heard of the 'tragedy of the commons' – an idea put forward by the late Garrett Hardin. In Hardin's view, the kind of co-operative commons I'm suggesting is just not something he thought could happen. It is against the kind of individual self-interest that has come to dominate economic and political thinking. However, the idea of a co-operative commons was championed by the late Elinor Ostram. Sometimes academics take pot-shots at one another through their writing, but Elinor took a different approach. There's a lovely story about her inviting Garrett Hardin around to her house for dinner. She made hot dogs. I don't know if hot dogs were a particular favourite of Garrett's or not, but his views did seem to change! Eventually he told us that it is an <u>unmanaged</u> commons that is the real tragedy. He was thereby implicitly accepting Elinor's work, which demonstrates that with the right governance in place a commons can be successful. Common land or other common resources can be owned by someone. The commons is not really about dividing everything, sharing everything or distributing everything equally. It's more about managing what is within our area of responsibility such that the resource, whatever it might be, is there for the long-term and such that everyone is treated fairly and such that nature is not destroyed but may even be enhanced by our activities.

Going back to the start of my story – why did those artists get so upset over the distribution of the little bit of money that came our way?

Well, artists – and especially those involved in what is described as 'socially-engaged art' – often have this notion of their work being a kind of cultural commons. And that idea is often linked to the further notion of a 'gift economy'. This takes a bit of unpacking. A gift economy is seen as the alternative to transactions and an alternative to a 'cost-benefit analysis' view of life. We're so used to hearing about the economy in terms of financial transactions that we forget there is a huge amount of co-operation and good will required to keep any kind of economy running. Capitalism would collapse without care – and care is a gift, the gift economy. So the gift economy is not something we need to aspire to – it already exists. Our socially-engaged work might then be to demonstrate that this is the case. To show that it is really care and compassion that keeps the world afloat even when we think it's capitalism.

But then that leads to a bit of a dilemma. If we are promoting 'the gift' then should we at the same time be asking for money for our efforts? It seems like a contradiction, and that's what caused our artists to get flustered over the finances. But really, it doesn't need to be this way. Of course we need our food, our clothes and a place to stay – and in a modern society most of this is achieved through money. But it can still be a 'gift economy'. There can be ownership and wages and transactions without all this destroying care, compassion, responsibility, service and reciprocity. That's a commons – or rather a whole series of commons working together within a larger society. It is a wholly different philosophy of life – one where the over-riding principles are the flourishing of individuals, communities, societies and nature. And all of that flourishing is not simply about exchanges of goods and services. A commons is to manage the gifts that nature and our fellow humans have bestowed on us. A commons is to get everything into balance and to live wisely. A commons is to help us to flourish and to let us work for the flourishing of others. If the city were a commons, what would you do?

If the City Were a Commons

In which the peculiarities of a real city lead to thoughts of how we might do better.

As I've mentioned, I had joined an arts project called 'If the city were a commons', based in the small city of Dundee on the East coast of Scotland. The Commons Group have gathered at a flat one of the artists is lucky enough to rent, down at the Waterfront in Dundee, overlooking the River Tay. It is a beautiful day and sunlight sparkles off the water. The coastline of Fife, over the river, is bathed in sunshine.

The Commoners have been asked to come up with a short statement of what each of us intends to contribute to the project over the coming months. We have gathered to share these ideas with each other. We have a walk around the Waterfront area as part of our day.

A cycle path runs along the river, through the Waterfront, but comes to an abrupt halt where it meets the docks. Anyone wishing to cycle further East, to Broughty Ferry and the beaches beyond, must double back to try and find a way out and around the docks. The Waterfront is littered with signs prohibiting various activities. Parking restrictions are especially onerous and confusing. One resident has received multiple parking tickets for leaving his car outside his own garage.

All of this is food for thought for the Commons Group. One person suggests building something at the farthest point of the Waterfront, so that, at least, the cyclists and walkers have some place to 'arrive' before they are forced to find a way back out. Could something be built without planning consent? The Waterfront path is arguably a public place, but should it really be a commons? If a commons, then why should permission have to be sought for a building? Another artist mentions a little piece of land further to the West and close to the Tay Rail Bridge. Perhaps this is genuinely common land? (We are investigating official common land in Dundee as part of the project.) Could we camp out on this site and draw attention to land use in the city?

After the walk around the Waterfront, further ideas are put forward. We discuss creating a proper beach at the Waterfront, stretching along to the city centre, instead of the mud and rocks that are there at the moment. There is talk of dancing and feasting. As the discussion goes on the ideas get ever-more fanciful. There's a sense of carnival that contrasts with the grim landscape of prohibitions that we've seen on our walk.

What would we do if we felt that we really owned our place, if the city was really ours, if the city were a commons?

What does it mean, first of all, to describe the city as a commons? It does not mean that there is no ownership or that everything becomes 'public' land (that is, owned and controlled by the state rather than privately). It's not who owns what that matters so much as what they do with what they own. A commons means that people living in a particular street, neighbourhood and region of our towns and cities would have a lot more say over what happens. This idea has come to be known as 'deliberative democracy' because small groups of people – local people, local communities – get together to deliberate over what's best for them. Good idea?

The downside is maybe that, just as in 'big' politics, only the people with money, power and influence get to see any changes made. There can be 'pocket tyrants' – mini dictators who push people around – at the local level just as much as national and international level. So deliberative democracy – neighbourhood councils and the like – are just encouraging bullies and busy-bodies to make trouble!

But I'd like to be more positive! I think it can work. I think the benefits – if we all had a chance to get involved – could really outweigh the disadvantages. Letting all voices be heard is what makes for a commons.

Cities are odd places. They say more about us than we might care to admit. The ancient city was often built around a sacred place such as a temple or a church. So the thing that was most important to people was placed at the centre. What matters most to us now, and how is that reflected in cities? Two things – autonomy and individuality. The autonomy is reflected in the design of infrastructure and our obsession with the car. Cities are now often just large intersections of roads and if they still have a centre at all then it will be a business district. Meanwhile commerce – shopping malls – are pushed out to the peripheries where they catch the road traffic. Traffic that might be going anywhere – anonymous, impersonal, autonomous. The individuality aspect is picked up in our homes. The modern house or apartment looks in on itself as a separate world that tends to shut out the surrounding location. It could almost be built anywhere, because it will do its best to shield us from the vagaries of the climate, the chaos of the local neighbourhood and the uncertainties of the world more generally.

So the modern city is based around people 'going places' (both literally and metaphorically) but when we are at home we are in our own private bubble. In fact, when we are at home we are probably still 'going places' by means of the internet and all we want is to shut out the surrounding neighbourhood so that we can pursue our own private dreams in peace. I'd add a third trend to this, which seems to be growing. We have started to make our physical places into fantasy places – theme parks. There is something adolescent starting to emerge in our cityscapes.

Well, if this is the way we really are as people then inevitably these are the kinds of places we're going to get for our urban landscape. But is this what we really want? I hope it isn't. I really hope it isn't!

Put the two parts of this together – the

commons and the city as a reflection of our ways as people – and we get a different view of what our urban landscape might be like. For if neighbourhoods and communities are the basis of a commons then the street and the neighbourhood would be the key element in how things were designed.

There would be small clusters of houses with parks and play areas, perhaps a pool, a sports field, some shops, a health clinic, a cinema, small business units, a vet, an optician – in short, all you need is on your doorstep. No need to drive to work, no need to seek out shopping malls or entertainment venues out of town. You could have a rich and happy life and not go more than three miles from your own door unless you really wanted to.

Instead of one big city centre – which might, in any case, have become an intersection of highways with some office blocks in between plus apartments no-one can afford – there would be multiple smaller centres for the regions of a city. These would be regions with their own history and identity and with some of the bigger stuff that cannot reasonably be provided at neighbourhood level. Again, we are reducing the need for transport – making things easier for ourselves and for nature. All it takes is careful planning. All it takes is to be careful of small details about what makes for a comfortable, happy life for everyone and not just for those who can afford it. All it takes is for enough of us to care enough to try. The 'intelligent' are not necessarily any better at this than the less intelligent, nor the richer any better than the poor.

You'll say perhaps that it's all very well to have dreams but people are just not like that. Most of us have given up trying to change the world, or even trying to change the neighbourhood, and all we can do is to retreat into our bubble and not bother anyone else.

I kind of agree. People would have to change first. People would have to genuinely want to be rooted in community rather than just pay lip-service to the idea, before genuine community would emerge. Meantime there's not much point in trying to physically build neighbourhoods as I've described them above, because unless people are on-message already then the places we build would not really work as places.

All I can say is, the city really could be a commons if we wanted it enough. And in the meantime, could we start living differently right where we are? Get to know the neighbours and the neighbourhood? Spread a little joy? Could you risk it?

Another Pudding is Possible

Holding Out for a Hero!

Politics, for the people, by the people!   Sounds fine, but...

To talk of politics is a difficult business. For one thing, a lot of the words and definitions used in political discussion keep shifting in their meanings – think, for instance, of terms like 'liberal', 'patriot', or 'progressive'. So I'm going to keep with a few very basic terms here, and I'm certainly not going to be digging into party politics. Instead I want to dig quite a bit deeper than any specific issues that might be around in political discourse today. For that, we can start by going back to one of the most basic of questions – why have government at all?
There are of course folks around who think we could do without a government of any kind, and indeed, that we could do without much or all of the institutions associated with government.

For this to work, there needs to be an extraordinary level of good will and engagement by all citizens of a nation. Are we up for that? Well, probably most of us would say no. But I think that idea of doing without a government is a good issue to raise nonetheless, because it gets us thinking about why we might need a government in the first place.

None of us really chose the political system that we are born into and governments generally don't make a habit of asking us whether or not the system we have is what we citizens actually want.

But it seems unlikely, let's face it, that if given a choice we would choose to have a monarchy (by which I mean a monarchy that actually wields power) or a dictatorship instead of a democracy.

Democracy though is a slippery term. We normally mean, for one thing, a government that is elected by free and fair elections. But that's not really a definition of a democracy – we could, after all, have elected to choose a dictatorship.

Democracy was originally rule by everyone. But it was on the scale of a city-state, and in theory every citizen could gather in some public place and give their opinion and then cast their vote for whatever decision was being discussed. Today we call that 'direct democracy', and whilst we now have nation-states as opposed to city-states, nonetheless, because of technology, we could in theory still have citizens debate and vote on all issues by way of referendums.

Maybe some of us would like this. After all, it gives most of us more of a say than we might ever hope to achieve under other systems.

But the arguments against such a system are ancient. For one thing, what if a whole population just came to a really bad decision? There is then no-one on the 'outside', as it were, to call the system to account for its mistakes. And what if some people – through great rhetoric or just personal charm – are just very much better at persuading others that their opinions are correct? Might not whole nations go off track as a result? The biggest worry with direct democracy though is that most people, most of the time, are not that inclined to be interested in the huge number of decisions that governments need to make, or to put in the necessary time and effort that would be needed to make informed decisions. Many of us realise that the world is a very complex place and we need experts to interpret what's going on. And many of us would prefer those experts to decide what's best to be done. So instead of direct democracy we have representative democracy.

We can think of that 'representative' part in a few different ways. The easiest way (and perhaps the way we might hope that it would work) is for our representative to listen to their electorate and come to some kind of balanced view about what we, the citizens, want or need. The alternative is that the representative (on the basis of being an expert) draws their own conclusions about what is best for us or for the nation as a whole and reaches decisions on this basis. And the third and more cynical view is that the representative is swayed by other forces – political parties, big business, rich donors – into making decisions that benefit those vested interests rather than serving the needs of the people.

The reality might be somewhere on a spectrum across these three options.

Well, let's step back a minute and take stock.

What if, miraculously, we were given a vote as to whether or not we wanted a government at all. And if we said yes to having a government then we were given further votes on exactly what kind of government we wanted. And let's say that, by an overwhelming majority, we still wanted a representative democracy. It would be very welcome to be given the choice! But my question now is, could there still be room for change within this system that we've all decided is best?

My answer is yes! And there are two sets of issues that I think are options for reform.

The first set of changes might best be described as 'constitutional reform'. We noted above that there is something of a spectrum in our representative democracy. There are representatives who truly have the will of the people and the good of the nation and of the planet at heart (plus the careful balance that needs to be struck between these three). At the other extreme there are 'representatives' who have their political careers and business interests at heart. Most of us (hopefully) would wish for more of the former and less (or none) of the latter. As I've said, the details of how this might be achieved could broadly be defined as constitutional reform. This, I'm sure it can be seen, is a whole lot more complex than simply choosing what kind of government we want – in terms of democracy instead of monarchy, for instance. It would take quite a level of engagement by citizens to get the kind of changes needed to achieve representatives who truly represent us. This level of engagement might be achieved by means of a partly 'bottom-up' style of governance. Such things as citizens' assemblies and deliberative democracy can feed into the broader political narrative so that all voices have the chance to be heard.

The second set of issues that might be further things to reform take us right back to that question of why we have governments in the first place. Here are four potential reasons:

For the safety and protection of citizens.

To allow all citizens to achieve their full potential – that is, to flourish.

To avoid gross disparities of wealth, such that all citizens regard society as organised fairly, so far as that is possible.

To protect the 'natural commons' of land, air and sea and the natural eco-systems that these support.

Reform, in respect of these four aims, would mean trying to get these aims more central to the decision-making of our representatives. You might of course disagree with some or all of these aims. Maybe the only place we could all agree is to say that there is some kind of absolute moral law that lies beyond human society and which we need to try to interpret in order to achieve good governance. I'd hesitate to say that I think any such absolute moral code really does exist. Introducing the idea of a philosophical or theological basis for morality and therefore governance might seem a very abstract notion. But actually, society itself does indeed have a background of shared moral value (however this has actually been derived) therefore it is not such an alien concept. People will, for instance, refer to some standard of fairness in discussions of all types, without (thankfully) having to justify where exactly this notion of fairness comes from!

If only, we might be thinking, things were not so polarised! If only there was more co-operation across the political spectrum. If only politicians treated each other with more respect! If only people listened to arguments and responded rationally and in terms of policy rather than merely reacting with aggression and personal insults! (But I have to say there is a certain sick voyeurism in the political fighting, back-stabbing, mud-slinging and abuse!)

You might say, given the way things are, we can but put forward our own views with a good deal of forcefulness and we should not see ourselves above deploying the kind of dirty tricks adopted by those who oppose us.

But, no! Granted, as things stand (and I'm thinking mainly UK and USA here) the types of constitutional reform I've described above seem desperately out of reach. But, call me naïve, I think that despite everything we are open to a story of a hero or a heroine to promote some of this change for us and as an alternative to the murky goings-on alluded to above. Such a one would be clear and forceful in their views, but would still treat their opponents with respect, no matter how despicable those opponents might actually be! So that is my modest hope – a political hero. Could we make it to at least that level of political competence? I hope. I hope....

Old Jim

In which memories of a misfit character prompt thoughts on community and power.

Old Jim was a memorable figure in my home town of Newport. He usually sported a shock of unruly hair and a full beard, but once a year he would go to the barber's and have it all cut off. It was strange to see him clean-shaven after this yearly ritual, his head bald and scabbed.

Old Jim could often be found outside the post office. Towards the middle of the day, sunlight reached in through the windows of the post office and alighted on the cleavage of the friendly young woman who worked behind the counter. Old Jim was transfixed. Surprisingly, the young woman would wave to Jim. Jim would give a nervous wave back, which only goes to prove that the correct behaviour around cleavages can be complex. Sometimes the

45

elderly post-mistress would come out of the shop and chase old Jim away.

Jim took refuge in the butcher's shop next door. Jim was not really the kind of person who could have found work, but Alan the butcher let him help out by chopping up meat and sometimes sawing up bones for the armies of pet dogs that belonged to the town and for those occasional folks who still prepare soup by boiling up a bone.

Jim could also be seen down by the river, staring out over the water. His oversized leather jacket would flap in the wind and his baggy jeans scuffed through the grass where he walked.

Jim's conversation was fairly basic, but he would always speak when he saw me. When you spoke to Jim he seemed to scrutinise you closely, as if looking for some sign that you were mocking him or holding him in contempt. Indeed, it became obvious that many people held a low opinion of him. Some would make shifty side-long glances at me as well, if they saw me stopping to speak with him.

Old Jim lived alone. One evening, whilst sitting in his armchair, he just slipped away to his eternal rest. In fact, it turned out that Jim had not been that old, being barely into his sixties when he died. When I lived in Newport I used to sit by the river myself quite often and I like to think that Jim could still somehow look down on the shifting waters of the River Tay. Who knows? Let's hope at least that he's keeping away from cleavages.

Every community has to face up to the issue of strange misfit characters in some way. Someone like Jim might have been locked up or driven away at one time. Now we are more inclined to try to include someone like Jim, even although it may be difficult for someone like him to really have a say in what his life should be like.

But someone like Jim, although they may appear problematic at times, is really one of the least worrying types of person we might encounter in small communities.

Let me explain further.

I heard a lovely story not long ago about a group of actors who had travelled to a small town to put on a show. The church hall had been left open for them so they could have a rehearsal ahead of the show in the evening. After the rehearsal they went through to the kitchen that adjoined the hall. Here they discovered three puddings – I think they were a lemon-meringue pie, a rhubarb tart and an apple crumble. The actors were delighted that the townsfolk had left them this generous gift and they fell to eating the puddings straight away. Just as they were finishing the last crumbs of the puddings a local woman came into the kitchen. She looked at the actors and at the empty plates, turned pale and walked out. She returned some minutes later with her husband in tow. The woman was too angry to speak so her husband spoke for her. 'These were for tonight', he said. The actors were mortified.

Well, we might ask, was it really such a big deal? Even although this was a small town, no doubt they had a store of some kind where more food could be purchased – or surely there was a supermarket not too far away from the little town. My suspicion though is that the woman was not really upset about the puddings! My suspicion is that there was some deeper problem in her life – maybe even one that she was not fully aware of – and that this was the real reason for her being upset. Why do I say this? The reason is that, having been part of numerous community groups, incidents like this are one of the most common occurrences. People will seem to be discussing some matter that the group needs to decide on, but in fact one or more people are actually talking about their own personal problems – their own buried hurts.

But there is another type of person even more toxic for groups. Think now about the really big political events you may have witnessed – something like a meeting of the G7 or a United Nations conference. Groups of presidents and prime ministers are there in front of the cameras and they are greeting each other. Here there is a kind of pecking order of apparently friendly gestures. One holds out his hand for a handshake, the other takes hold of it with two hands and then it's very difficult for either one to let go! Whoever lets go first, you see, is the one who will appear to be slightly less friendly. So there's a bit of a competition as to who appears the most open and welcoming. The same thing happens with the hugs. After a bit of a hug then one party will move onto patting the other one on the back. Then the other must start patting and then who is going to be the first to break the hold and stop the patting? The message here is that powerful people play strange games, and this applies in small groups just as much as it does amongst world leaders and politicians. Any group may have someone, or several people, so sure of their own opinions that it does not even occur to them that they could ever be wrong. If someone were to challenge their authority then the powerful person will often just find this confusing – there is no notion that they might have been misunderstood or that they might need to change their minds. And it can be even worse in groups that aspire to some kind of equality amongst its members – the powerful person, the pocket tyrant, will actually believe that they are sticking with the group's ethos of equality whilst all the while making life very difficult for everyone else.

Old Jim knew he wasn't clever and knew that he relied on other people for help. The woman with the puddings might one day have realised that all her more petty concerns were because of some deep hurt within her and she might have found a way of healing that hurt. But alas it is very difficult for the pocket tyrant ever to back down – very difficult, but still, sometimes, it happens.

These matters are sometimes expressed in terms of power relations. 'Power-over' is the relation we have just been discussing – the domain of the pocket tyrant. Groups might aim instead for 'power-with' – that is, shared power. But that can be a mistake. People cherish their power and won't give it up easily. Even the lady with the puddings and people like her have a certain kind of power because in a way they can hold a group to ransom. The group is not giving them the attention they crave. They secretly want the group to sympathise with them and even to try to solve their problems for them, so in the meantime they hold the group to ransom by disrupting whatever is going on and attempting to turn the spotlight back to their own personal issues.

A further alternative in power relations is

sometimes referred to as 'brokenness'. That's not supposed to mean that the community or group is destroyed. It means rather that people let down their barriers, admit to their own failures, accept a loss of dignity and not take themselves too seriously but instead be able to see the humour in themselves. To be humble.

We might call this state of 'brokenness' a form of 'power-under', because it collapses all of the power games of power-over and even of power-with (where the workings of power are really still bubbling away beneath the surface). Power-under is a tricky term because it is sometimes used to mean a resentment of the powerful but at the same time a certain welcoming of having a routine and having people telling us what to do. But I don't mean it in that sense. I mean it rather as a conscious refusal to accept any power relations. Let's face it, community groups, workplace meetings and communities can be boring affairs at times. But if a group can get itself to that power-under state then it starts to be a place where we can truly be ourselves and in fact to know ourselves more fully because of the relationships amongst the group. Power-under sees the beauty, the poetry and the humour in life and relationships. It sees life as the artist would see it – and we can all be artists.

These days of course we can just about avoid any kind of group if we choose to – we can run away from our families, leave our jobs and not attend any kind of community gathering. The message of contemporary Western culture is of the autonomous and self-sufficient individual. And if there were some major upheaval to life – a nuclear war, the end of world trade, the destruction of the internet, the collapse of government – then our 'solution' is what is often described as 'survivalist'. We might choose to 'bug-in', that is, guard our own homes and have sufficient means to survive there for at least the short to medium-term. Or otherwise, we might plan to 'bug-out', that is, to run for shelter in some remote spot where we have a stash of food and supplies or where we might forage or hunt.

All of this rather smacks of desperation, and of course it is very much a young person's game. The elderly, the disabled, those needing ongoing medical care – well, they are just left to die. Instead, I'd suggest, true resilience comes through community. And of course it is very much the broken, power-under kind of community I have in mind here. So, my suggestion, if you really want to survive whatever disaster might come our way, is to get to know your neighbours! And even if there is no terrible disaster in the immediate future, building community is still a brilliant thing to be engaged with. Politics can be something of a dirty word these days. But politics, to get back to its original meaning, is just about how we as people organise ourselves. Politics starts with the street.

Your street might have an old Jim, a lady with worries she cannot quite confess or a pocket tyrant. But power under is possible. Why not give it a go!

Anger, Biscuits and Voices of Dissent

In which the author uses biscuits to quieten his father - and a particular biscuit incident leads to thoughts on dissenting voices!

My Dad always had a habit of shouting at the television. When I was a child of course these outbursts meant nothing to me. I had since returned home – in my late 50's – to be his carer. I have to say that at this stage I was still none the wiser as to what his shouts at news and current affairs programmes actually meant! So I chose not to question his outbursts, so as to maintain domestic harmony! And in these later years of course I had the wherewithal to offer him a biscuit to try and shut him up!

One particular event stays in my mind. A political programme on TV was hosting a rather controversial figure in British politics. I sensed an outburst from Dad at any moment, so I fetched him a biscuit. But oddly he remained silent all through the TV interview and debate – the biscuit poised half way between plate and mouth.

So there it was – a voice of dissent on TV, and so controversial that nothing like it has really been aired since. So shocking it even shut up my Dad!

It leads me to thinking about how much we should tolerate dissent. One of the trickiest questions in politics and indeed in morality is, should we tolerate the intolerant? Should we accept people with extreme views, such as that person I had watched with my Dad that night?

It's not a question that lends itself to a yes or no answer. On the yes side, we might say that society should value free speech, freedom of the press and the like. On the no side, we might say that a line needs to be drawn where free speech becomes abuse, harassment or incitement to violence. So that's the thing. There needs to be a line drawn somewhere, but where do we draw it? We might all offer different opinions and somehow society as a whole needs to make a judgement about where the line is drawn on a society-wide basis. I'd suggest that the line needs to be constantly watched and constantly re-negotiated, as media, opinion and circumstances change so rapidly.

This matter then – the matter of dealing with intolerance – is a troubling area of politics in general because it challenges the very foundations of what politics is supposed to be addressing. Here's five potential foundations for what government is about:

For the safety and protection of citizens.

To allow all citizens to achieve their full potential

– that is, to flourish.

To avoid gross disparities of wealth, such that all citizens regard society as organised fairly, so far as that is possible.

To protect the 'natural commons' of land, air and sea and the natural eco-systems that these support.

And the fifth: The form of government itself should be open to review by citizens – that is, for most countries – the constitution should be negotiable by the electorate.

Well of course someone might bitterly disagree with some or all of these notions. Not only that, someone might see the stated aims of government as being a cover for a different agenda! So we have our dissenting voices – what do we do?

I'm not going to try to defend the rationality of the aims given above, or indeed the stated aims of any actual government or political party. To do that would lead us perhaps to a fractured debate that might result in the different 'sides' becoming just more entrenched in their opinions.

Instead, can we just agree that some political views, whatever they may be, are controversial, challenging, unorthodox? And if we agree this point, then all I'd venture to ask is, why do some people hold views of this type? Why do some people choose to be off the mainstream, dissenting voices?

In answer to this, the first thing to say is that these are generally not bad people. They may be angry, controversial and outspoken, but not bad. The reason I say this is that, for the most part, bad people are just not interested in politics! So they're not likely to have an opinion either way, let alone seek a platform for their opinions. But of course history has delivered us with plenty of notable exceptions! So it can be easy for us to brand people whose opinions we find deeply upsetting as deranged psychopaths! But I urge you to consider that this is probably not true! No matter how objectionable the opinions might be, there is likely to be some genuine motive at the root of why people defend the opinions and political views that they have come to hold.

So our second step is to consider the deeper reasons behind those controversial views.

Let's say that there is some 'higher truth' that is being sought. This makes sense since – if the stated aims of government (or society at large) seem to be suspicious or just outright wrong – then there must be some higher truth that is brought to bear in order to challenge the mistakes. What might that higher truth be? Well, I mention fairness in the brief summary of a government's aims. But there it is a limited form of fairness – simply amounting to an equitable (though not necessarily equal) distribution of resources. We might first of all disagree and say that a government should not try to impose some kind of financial re-distribution or we might disagree the other way and say that the government should aim for a much more equal society. But behind all this, fairness might be considered a much wider value than this, and rightly so. Of all moral ideas, fairness is the one that could most reasonably claim to be 'innate' – that is, we are more or less born with a sense of fairness and it is beyond human ingenuity to argue for some more basic standard by which to measure right and wrong. Even – I would hazard to say – those who believe in God would never, ever accept someone claiming that God does not act fairly!

So my contention here is that sooner or later, in any debate, one side will say that what the other side is proposing is not fair. Then the other side will respond in kind, that is, with a counter-argument based on fairness.

We might well be horrified by what some people consider to be fair. But even so, the question still comes down to fairness. Look again at the five ideas around government mentioned earlier. We could re-frame all of them as fairness arguments:

It's fair that governments protect us (because, for instance, we pay our taxes).

It's fair that all citizens should be able to flourish (because all people are valuable in and of themselves).

It's fair that there should be an equitable distribution of resources (because everyone has the right to at least a reasonable standard of living, but at the same time people with outstanding ability or who work exceptionally hard deserve to be rewarded).

It's fair that we protect the environment. (Because we ultimately rely on nature for everything and if we destroy her we will likely destroy human life as well. And because animals and plants have a claim over nature as well as humans.)

It's fair that the way society is governed is open for review by its citizens.

And so, with any discussion, no matter how bizarre the claims that are being made, we can find fairness lurking behind them.

But now the really tricky bit! Sometimes it may be possible to argue people around to a different point of view (and this means essentially convincing them that their way of understanding fairness has been mistaken in some way). But when it comes to more extreme views, no amount of reasoned debate or shouting is going to work! The more extreme the view the more strongly its proponents will cling to it, because it is just too costly to give in – to give in would be to lose face in a big way!

So how might they be persuaded, if we are of a mind to try?

Some of you reading this aren't going to like my answers here! But hey! I hope you'll give me a hearing.

First of all, give up any notion of trying to change the other person's mind! That's right, persuasion just ain't going to work! So give it up. Instead, just shut up and listen. Listening to other people gives them dignity – the dignity all of us deserve (even people we find obnoxious!). Then wait. There's no need to ask any questions, because the person with strong opinions will be only too ready to share them with you! There's going to be an unfairness message buried somewhere in amongst the rhetoric. And here's the crucial part. It might be that the argument boils down to a straight-forward case of <u>political</u> unfairness – by which I mean some unfairness in society, in which case they may be open to some discussion about what fairness should mean. But it may be that the 'unfairness' is some kind of personal hurt or grievance. Or the two may be mixed. Should we point out the personal hurt behind the political rhetoric? Unless they have become a close friend I'd say certainly not! Just listen and listen and listen, because eventually someone can talk their way into seeing things differently just through their own talking. If they cannot talk, then, as with most of us, our thoughts cannot move forward.

All of this that I've said above is really about one-to-one, in person conversations. There is a whole different matter of addressing people who hold political office. If we want our views to be heard then firstly acknowledge that this is the current set-up – they are in power and you are not. And secondly, our argument is never with the person (even if their personal life may be highly dubious) but with their actions within government and/or their policies as a government or an opposition party. So be polite, straight-forward, rational and keep to the point. This much should be obvious. But clearly it is happening less and less. As we are given greater and greater access to our leaders through social media so the levels of abuse that they suffer grow exponentially.

My further thought then is whether to engage with these so-called 'trolls'? What motivates the troll? Well they may be those people with extreme viewpoints that we have been discussing up until now. If they want their views heard properly then verbal abuse of serving politicians is not the way to go about it. It's more likely however that they have a grievance with life rather than with politics. Trying to have an online conversation with such a person is going to be very difficult indeed. Given the violence and abuse of many posts by trolls, we cannot easily intervene. The angry person will never admit that their anger is coming from hurt. But, as someone has said, we harm others by our unexamined pain. I am grateful to one of my online followers for pointing out that sometimes people have opinions that barely make it to the level of conscious thought – it is all emotion. And therefore trying to have a debate with someone like this is not going to work. We'd need to reach them on some emotional level rather than a rational level. Encountering someone like this in real life though can be a daunting prospect! Best back away slowly and then run like hell! But if listening is an option, then this at least might offer a place of peace – and that, potentially, can communicate at the emotional level. But clearly, none of that can work for the online troll.

If we cannot really tackle the angry troll and our voices are necessarily modest and quiet when we approach someone holding political office, then, you may be thinking, there's not much left for us! But I'd venture to say that the polite listening and the forging of friendships with neighbours and work colleagues is actually a very powerful force! Every day there are millions of conversations. So, what if we make our conversations ones where we listen carefully, look for the fairness issues, look for the underlying hurt and then simply bear witness to the way other people see the world? Don't argue, don't offer advice, just listen.

Rice Pudding Culture

A paddy field leads to the overthrow of capitalism... Okay, well, perhaps not yet!

Imagine, if you will, a paddy field of rice ready for harvest. The nearby village has plenty of workers willing and able to bring in the harvest. If they press ahead with their work then everyone can eat.

Such a simple model of subsistence farming is often given to show that societies can function without money, or indeed, without capitalism.

But then comes a 'but'! For those writers who are looking to celebrate the benefits of the capitalist system, a market economy, or some such, then the 'but' might take the form of: But what if there's a drought or a hurricane or a flood? Hence, the subsistence farmer is vulnerable to disaster. Or it might be simply to say: But what if the farmers want to buy a truck, or go see a film, or gain access to the internet? Hence, there are things that a small group of people cannot do for themselves. So a more complex system of exchange – trade, money, debt – is a way that people gain access to a wider range of goods and services.

On the other hand, those with a grudge against capitalism will use the paddy field and its workers to show a different set of concerns. They may, for instance, say: But what if the workers wanted a higher wage for bringing in the harvest? They are saying therefore that 'the system' (that is, a system of waged labour) might fail even with an abundant harvest and a plentiful supply of labour because the pay does not match the aspiration of the workers. The point is that all we need is actually there for the taking, but there is an 'economic failure'. Hence, and this is their point, we might be surrounded by abundance but our system of economics – capitalism, market economies, waged labour – fails us.

Well, who is right? As usual, with this kind of complex question, no-one is really right or wrong. Life is not so simple. But the example of the paddy field might help us make a bit of sense of the complex issues around capitalism, and indeed, the way we choose to organise societies generally.

Let's unpack that a bit.

First of all, let's be certain that we are surrounded by an abundance. For the most part we think of this as an abundance of material resources. But remember the example again. There is also an abundance of workers. And where did they come from? Well, of course they came from their mothers! So they ultimately came from Mother Nature – the same source as our material resources. And they also came from a good deal of care and support from family, friends, schools and the like. This is the more hidden aspect of our equation, which goes by a variety of names. Let's just call it care here, for simplicity.

So those folk who argue that life would be possible without all the problems of capitalism are partly right – because there is indeed an abundance provided by nature and an abundance of care that allows for an abundance of people to do the work that can then sustain us. We could thrive just by seeing all this abundance as gifts – a gift economy. We could make sure that everything we made could be re-used or recycled – a circular economy. But yes (I know you're already thinking) it's a tough call! Because most of us want to do a whole lot more than grow fruit and vegetables!

Capitalism has already delivered a lot of those extras that our subsistence farmers might aspire to – the comfortable homes, the cars, the gadgets, international trade and travel. But of course it has its problems, which even the most enthusiastic advocates of consumer capitalism are forced to admit. Two problems are most apparent – capitalism is based on growth and capitalism is based on debt. The two problems are closely linked. Capitalism is based on borrowing the means by which production is increased and it's the compound interest on that borrowing which is the main source of debt. To keep paying the debt there needs to be more and more production, so more and more natural resources must be used up in order to keep the system going.

Fans of capitalism don't necessarily have a problem with this. We could simply say that there will always be new natural resources, either from the Earth, or eventually from the moon, or Mars or the asteroid belt. And this expansion could go on and on, to other star systems, other galaxies and even other universes!

Another way to look at it is to say that economic growth does not have to rely on natural resources. There is an argument that says it could be the cultural industries or the financial economy that allow for growth, without us plundering the natural world any more than we do already. Hence, we could be environmentally sustainable but economically growing.

It's a neat idea, but I doubt that it's true. Cultural industries still rely on nature and finance is still ultimately based on the idea that someone, somewhere will eventually pay debts, and this will be by way of work and hence based on the material economy.

An alternative would be to recognise we are reliant on the material economy and to work towards making this truly sustainable. As mentioned earlier, this could be by way of what's called a 'circular economy'. In other words, instead of expanding where we look for new materials we make sure that everything we do in our making and manufacturing is done such that we can repair things or recycle them by the most efficient means possible. Nature of course is the ultimate circular economy. We can look to her and imitate her ways. But, fair to say, whilst this would greatly help our world, it does not, by itself, stop the expansion of material resources needed to sustain economic growth.

Another way to look at it is to ask if we could have capitalism without either growth or debt.

This seems at least a viable alternative. Part of the reason it's viable is that when we talk of growth we normally mean economic growth and this in turn normally means goods and services plus finance. When we talked about the workers and their field of rice, we noted another kind of economy that I've called care, which sits below the horizon but nonetheless supports everything we do. Could we pay more attention to care and thereby see societies flourishing even whilst our material prosperity remains much the same from year to year?

Well, here's a few thoughts on what that might mean. There are three.

Firstly we might ask what 'the economy' – all that making and doing, buying and selling, trading and bartering – is really for? We might be tempted to reply, for profit! But really, the answer should be, for service. We serve our needs by having a job and earning money. And we serve the needs of society through our trades and professions. We might see this 'service' as simply meeting our material needs. But we might expand this to include the wider goal of each of us achieving some kind of flourishing in our lives. To flourish is not just to have our material needs met, but also our needs of relationship, education, culture and more besides.

That takes us to our second thing. Seeing everything through the lens of economics has the tendency to reduce everything to a transaction of some sort – a cost-benefit analysis of what may best meet our needs. Everything then has been commodified, meaning that it has value only in so far as it can be exchanged. The alternative to this is to recognise that some things have worth rather than value. Or to put it another way, they are important to us just for what they are in themselves – they have intrinsic worth. No doubt we very much hope this is true of ourselves as persons! We are more than what we might earn from our work and more than just our physical selves. And likewise for much else in life – the natural world, good health, relationships, culture. So part of growth that is not economic growth (and part of the growth that is in fact part of human flourishing) is to appreciate all those things in life that have intrinsic worth rather than transactional value.

And thirdly, let's think again about the idea of a gift economy we mentioned earlier. Sometimes gift economies are thought of as a return to bartering or some kind of 'reciprocity'. But if we see them in this way we're really stuck with the kind of cost-benefit transactional mind-set we looked at above. We said nature's abundance is a gift and we said too that the care we give and receive from others is a gift. These things are in the realm of intrinsic worth, not transaction. When we are serving others through our work or giving ourselves to others through our care, this is gifting in its truest sense.

But we can go even a step further and remember that it is part of every healthy person's life to seek 'flourishing' in whatever ways that makes sense for each individual. Putting this all together we could describe the gift economy as 'enhancing the gifts of others'. In other words, we are not just giving our work and our care blindly. We are instead being very specific in understanding what will help particular people, particular communities, and particular places (both natural and human-made) to flourish.

So the workers in the field might bring in their rice harvest and have their simple meal of rice and be satisfied – because there is so much more going on in their lives. Or, on the other hand, a complex technological culture may learn to live within its natural limits and likewise thrive. Because human flourishing and helping each other to flourish could be our true aims.

Do I think this is possible? Yes! Do I think it's going to happen? No! For a developed nation to step outside the usual pattern of economic growth is, in a sense, to bring the nation to its knees! The value of their currency would plummet, their borrowing costs would sky-rocket and their stock exchange would collapse! Any government trying to bring in such changes would therefore be very quickly out of office and there would then be a mad scramble to get the economy back on its capitalist growth track. It has to be said that such change may be forced onto us via a fuel crisis, war, a collapse in world trade or as a result of runaway climate change. Or a combination of all of these. Of course I wouldn't welcome this enforced change, because the truth is most of us are just not ready for the scale of change that all of the above would entail. As such, it would not, as things stand, result in a peaceful life of subsistence farms, eco-villages and peaceful people seeking flourishing and enchantment! No, it would be carnage! Even if we chose a hi-tech future, the risks of the kind of global collapse I mention are equally problematic. We could end up with pockets of hi-tech privilege in amongst an outer world of chaos and violence.

So my conclusion is that we have to change as people in order to cope with the kinds of problems the world may throw at us in the coming decades. And I include myself in that need for change. It's just not something big government can bring about. Big government (and indeed, local governance) could go some way towards shielding us from some of the problems coming down the track. The sort of problems we're all aware of – like climate change and fuel shortages and the consequences these things are likely to have. But governments can't change people – we need to be the change.

In the light of all this, I keep my hopes for the future modest! I hope that we survive as a species. I hope that in the very long-term people will start to see life differently. We could have a sustainable world. We could live in harmony with nature. We could be peace-loving, committed to care, serving others, multiplying the gifts of others. It seems, right now, like a faint hope, but I'm going to try keeping it alive.

Back to Nature

In which strange encounters in a sauna lead to thoughts on wild body, wild mind, wild soul…!

The Commons Group has been invited to visit an 'art installation' at a Dundee gallery, just before its official opening to the public. The installation was essentially a sauna, constructed from a polythene greenhouse and a couple of wallpaper strippers that produced steam. The idea of the installation was to see if people would be more sociable when they met with few or no clothes and thus with most of the usual clues to status removed. I suspect that those who put the installation together hadn't met British people before!

The visit was arranged for just after our regular meeting and noticeably most people made a very sharp exit when the regular meeting concluded! It was only four of us who made our way down the street to the gallery. This was our Commons group leader, his partner, another female friend and me. The sauna had been made ready for us and was certainly warm and steamy.

Us guys were in our underwear. The women had taken everything off, but were wrapped in big white fluffy towels. Given that we all knew each other quite well already, it's difficult to judge whether conversation was easier in this state of undress. We were relaxed. There was however a bit of an intrusion when a few other members of the Commons Group showed up and bundled into the sauna fully clothed. They had the decency to feel out of place and quickly left.

My female friend gave me a lift home after the sauna visit and we chatted about our experiences of nudity. It turned out we had both visited the seaside resort of Biarritz in France, where attitudes to bare flesh are a good deal more relaxed than in the UK. In Biarritz, sure enough, it is the naked people who are the most friendly.

We sometimes use the phrase, 'going back to nature' when we talk about people being nude. It's a telling phrase. There's clearly a strong connection in our minds between our bodies and the natural world that surrounds us. And I suspect that if someone loves nature then chances are they're comfortable with their bodies and likewise someone relaxed in their own skin may well be a nature lover.

It's a personal thing, but nudity brings to mind both the beauty of the human body and also our frailty and vulnerability. We may not all be equal by any means in our physical appearance, but the pleasures and pains of the flesh are certainly common to us all. I think our humanity is very much about nature and our connection to her through our bodies.

So I love the term 'wild body' because it helps to make clear that strong link between our physical selves and the rest of nature. Humans, to me, are wild of body, wild of mind and wild of soul. But of course, in our modern societies especially, we don't get to see much of this wildness. People keep their bodies covered up – as we've been discussing – but also the wild mind gets squashed from a young age by education. Education geared towards particular kinds of learning designed to make passive citizens suitable for the kind of dull and restrictive employment we're offered once we're grown! And what of wild soul? What does that even mean to us in a world that often denies such a thing as a soul even exists? So we're very much on our own and swimming against the tide if we want to care for our souls in a modern society.

The three types of wild – wild body, wild mind, wild soul – are closely linked. We need a certain kind of wild mind in order to seek out wilderness in the world. And it is nature's wildness that helps to feed our wild souls.

But nature is in trouble. We humans are taking up more and more space – for cities, roads and railways as well as farming, forestry and fishing. Thus, if we want to find ourselves a wild place to go and be with nature then we may well face a longer and longer journey. How far is it for you to the mountains or the beach, the forest or a lake? And of course getting there probably means a car, a train or even a plane – so we add to the problem. Setting aside all questions of pollution or climate change, loss of bio-diversity, over-fishing and acidification of the oceans – it is this loss of natural places that is somehow closest to our hearts.

Wild nature calls out to our wild bodies, wild minds and wild souls. When we hurt, nature is hurt. When nature is hurt we are hurt. If we could heal ourselves we could start healing nature. And healing nature would mean solving all those other problems – climate change and the like – along the way.

Okay, so I know that if you're 'on message' with regard to climate and all those other issues, then you're probably thinking more along the lines of electric cars and solar panels! But I'd say that such things are, in a way, just more of the same – more development, more natural resources used up, more wilderness destroyed, in order to have a 'sustainable' economy. I don't mean that such effort is not well-intentioned. I just mean that behind all of this is the wild nature that we must rely on. Why not go straight to her and heal her rather than trying to find ways to live without her (which is what a lot of technology is really about).

So what to do? Well, I'm all for activism, to save the rainforests and other natural environments, not just for their beauty, but because we rely on them for everything. (Even if we go to live on Mars, we will have to take some of Earth's nature with us in order to survive.) But activism isn't for everyone – and besides, activism or not, we need to be living our message in our own lives.

So if wild body, wild mind and wild soul mean anything at all then we have to somehow live them. Sometimes – in fact, a lot of the time – this means doing stuff that does not seem to directly relate to the problems we've been discussing. But I'd counter this by saying, wilderness is infectious!

What of wild body? In our modern Western culture it's not just the appearance of our bodies that is problematic. The body has a whole life of its own and very often our minds are almost totally unaware of what our bodies are feeling – the way our bodies see the world. Certainly there are, for instance, such things as psychosomatic illnesses – that is, the mind affecting the body. This might suggest the mind is in charge. But in fact it is the body that is largely in charge of our lives, even whilst it struggles to be heard above the clamour of our minds! So we should try listening to our bodies! Such things as tiredness, headaches and tension in our muscles are signs that the body is not entirely happy with the way we're living our lives. Believe me when I say there is no way around this! The body is in charge! If we don't listen to our bodies and figure out what needs to change then sooner or later things will get worse. Eventually bodies will shut us down until they get what they need!

When it comes to other people it's helpful to remember the same scenario is being played out with them – their bodies are in charge but they are in denial! Their bodies will determine how they relate to us (and we'll respond in kind). So there is no use denying our instant affection or dislike for other people! We might cover this over with polite conversation, but let's not forget the underlying reality! Things can change, of course. But it is not the mind that will convince the body that we should like someone, or whatever. The body will find her own way, in her own time.

Even on a community and societal scale, the body is key. All politics is actually the politics of the body. Whatever policy a government may have about such things as defence, economics, immigration, education – these are all ultimately about the effects on bodies. It's bodies that provide the hidden economy of care that undergirds all societies. It's bodies that provide the labour element of production in our material economy. It's bodies, ultimately, that create culture. No matter how much we develop robotics and artificial intelligence, no matter how much culture becomes abstract and virtual, these things can never escape the body. Bodies who feel pleasure and pain. Bodies who have emotion. Bodies that are truly alive. Bodies are the only means through which dreams can be fulfilled.

What of wild mind? Well you might be thinking a 'wild mind' sounds like a crazy mind, and isn't there enough craziness in the world without encouraging more! But no, I'd prefer to think of wild mind as meaning 'free mind' rather than crazy mind. What does that freedom consist of? Well, it's about asking questions like: What do I really want my life to be about? Am I really making my own choices or am I just trying to impress people? Will the story of my life be one that I can be proud of when I'm old or am I just drifting along without any clear goals in mind? The wild free mind thinks out of the box on all of these issues.

What of wild soul? To speak of wild soul seems like something amazingly psychedelic! I don't want to disparage psychedelia – and there may, for instance, be times when we benefit greatly from stepping back from life for a while and gaining a wider perspective. But we cannot escape from the world forever. If soul has any meaning at all then it has to be dealing with our everyday familiar world. Soul – if this does not seem like too outlandish a claim – is about seeing the ordinary world as enchanted. It's only in this way that the soul can inspire the mind and bring pleasure and contentment to the body.

Well, dear reader, you might not believe in souls and you might find this talk of enchantment bizarre and nonsensical! Okay, well try telling someone they don't have a soul! Somehow we all believe in an intrinsic self, even although we cannot say exactly what it is. And as for enchantment – I don't mean some big revelation or some blinding flash that suddenly makes everything seem different. No. Life, for the most part, is made up of millions of tiny events. If we're to find enchantment we have to look for it in the small stuff. And it starts that way – by looking – really looking and spending some time letting events settle into our minds and hearts. That's where body, mind and soul really meet up – in that contemplation of the small stuff of life.

So I like to think of wild soul seeing beauty right where it is. The park, the garden, the birds – these are all contacts with wild nature. The crazy fashions, the smiles and the humour – these are all contacts with our fellow humans. The little acts of kindness, just being there as a reliable, honest and consistent presence, the word of advice we can offer when asked – these are all small gifts of grace we can bring to the world. All of that adds up to a lot. That's wild soul. That's daring to be ourselves!

To have a soul is to have a bit of wisdom. And to have a bit of wisdom probably means seeing the world as a very crazy place! When we see the craziness of the world there is a tendency to get involved somehow – to try to fix things.

This is a difficult one – should we stick with the small stuff, or should we get involved with the big issues around the world? You may be feeling an irresistible compulsion to be an activist on some issue! In which case, it's difficult for me to suggest you should resist! All I can say is, can we have both? Activism inspired by wild soul? I leave that one with you! Are we sorted then? Have we managed to capture wild nature by discussing wild body, wild mind and wild soul? Not yet, I suspect! The problem is that we are part of nature but also we stand outside her – such is the position of self-consciousness. And we can never 'unthink' it – we can almost never experience the wild directly and so respond straight from body, mind and soul. Instead, we will always place ourselves in hypothetical situations of either the future or the past. What if we did this? What if that hadn't happened? What if? What if? We cannot help but analyse and therefore we always feel ourselves to be on the outside of circumstances, looking in. We could stubbornly argue that this is okay and we are still nature. But whether we do this or not, we could stop to ask, is there really a problem? Is self-consciousness really a curse, so far as nature is concerned, or could it be a blessing?

If a blessing then I think we'd have to say this is about our relationship with nature. To say we have a relationship with nature is already to acknowledge that we stand apart from her, as we've explored above. But what we bring to nature through self-consciousness can still be a positive – in fact, we will not have that enchantment of nature I spoke of earlier without some of this standing apart. Let's unpack that a little.

The tendency these days is to regard nature as being about co-operation and mutual aid. People who promote this view have presumably never been chased by a lion or a bear! I'd rather say that we see all human emotion – both beautiful and terrible – reflected back to us when we look at nature. All of nature is in turn reflected in our own natures.

Given this, I think the conclusion must be that we'll always feel at least a little ambiguous when it comes to nature. And ambiguity does not need to be a bad thing! To love nature is not just to see her beauty but also to embrace her ambiguities. To love ourselves is likewise to accept ambiguity. We cannot be perfect – we are all flawed vulnerable humanity – but still we can love. In fact it is often flaws and vulnerability which give us the greatest moments of love and of enchantment. When we spend time with nature we are reminded of all these strange parallels in our own lives.

We are led to believe that one day we could take a human brain and put it into an artificial body or that we could one day upload a conscious mind into a computer. Detached therefore, completely from nature, what kind of life would that be? If it proves to be possible at all then I'd have to say this would not be a human life. It's easy to think that someone living in a city who spends all their time looking at screens is already half way towards just being a mind inside a computer! Perhaps you think your teenage son is already somewhat more than half way! But we breathe air, there are dozens – maybe hundreds – of other species of creature that live on and inside us, we eat mostly biological foodstuffs, even when highly processed, and we interact with other humans.

Our immersion in nature is therefore more or less absolute, even in a city. There is no life without nature – there is no 'us' without her. So let's give up on these fantasies of living without her and instead find ways to be with her more. Let's embrace her, reflect her within ourselves and see ourselves written in her.

Another Pudding is Possible

Some Thoughts on Compassion

In which the author offers tea and cake to a distraught friend and considers the link between small and large-scale compassion.

Some of us in the Commons Art Group have gone along to a dance performance called 'Plan B for Utopia' (which subsequently featured at the Edinburgh Fringe Festival). One of those attending is a friend called Joanna. I suggest we might go for a cup of tea to talk about the Plan B performance, and she agrees.

I was very short of money in those days. However, I'm an old-fashioned kind of person and still feel it's a gentleman's prerogative to buy for a lady. Every woman is a descendant of the Queen of Sheba, I've since told Joanna on many occasions, and the Queen of Sheba doesn't pay for her own chai and chowder. (I think I learnt this fact from pop legend, Sister

Sledge.)

There is an anxious moment however, as Joanna considers having a salad. It costs more than I have in cash and I don't know if any of my bank cards will work. Luckily, she settles instead for a slice of lemon drizzle cake along with her tea. I have enough for a cuppa myself, with only pennies left.

Joanna seems anxious and before long a story of recent troubles in her life starts to unfold. I glance nervously at the time as Joanna's story continues. Eventually, I must apologise and step out of the café to phone my Dad and say that the evening meal will be delayed. This news is equivalent to telling him that he must lose an arm. I suggest that he visits the biscuit tin to tide him over until I return home.

Back in the café and Joanna is sobbing heavily. I find myself tongue-tied, so try simply to make encouraging grunts. Somehow, Joanna interprets this as reassurance. The trauma passes. Joanna's face brightens. It seems like talking things through has been cathartic.

I reach home and dinner is delivered one hour and ten minutes late. Dad appears distraught. He had found the biscuit tin but been unable to open the lid. Soon though, he settles, and the normal routine of dinner and watching the news on TV is re-established. When I find time to myself I have a long think over the story Joanna has told me. What is most striking is that she seems to have no condemnation or judgement against the people who have wronged her. On the other hand, perhaps she is silently fuming and just not admitting it. Perhaps she secretly longs to smash something over the heads of her antagonists. Or perhaps, as the Queen of Sheba, she might wish to sell them into slavery, have them put into cages, slung over the back of a camel and carried off to some unknown fate.

Maybe, I think, it would be better if she was really angry – although best not with the smashing things or the selling into slavery. When it comes to situations like this, the feelings get complicated.

I send an email off to Joanna to check she has reached home safely. Then it's tea and biscuits with Dad and off to bed.

That question – whether to forgive someone and let things go, or whether to take a stand and express our anger – is a dilemma we all face from time to time. Anger is a frightening emotion and sometimes we would prefer just to smooth things over rather than express the anger we are feeling. But then the anger can fester until it finds expression in some unsuitable ways, such as outbursts towards people who don't deserve our wrath. And this can often be over matters not even connected with the original cause of the upset. Anger can also be the expression of something else – grief, fear, despair – so again the person who might be the target of an angry outburst might be the unsuspecting bit-player in a drama that is really about some deeper hurt within us.

All of this leads me to think that we need to be very slow in reacting to difficult circumstances. We are best to buy time, somehow, to think through how we really feel and then find a way to carefully explain where things stand with those involved.

The surprising thing in all this is how much the big scale of societies and nations relate to the small-scale world of our own families, friends and workplaces. Our nation, for instance, may stockpile weapons and give out very clear signals that any threats to our sovereignty will be met with severe reprisals. And our nation might do very little for the poor and vulnerable in our society. So a lack of compassion is the default response. Such big politics are usually beyond our control, but these policies, I think, filter down to the smaller concerns of our everyday lives. When the nation threatens its enemies and fails to care for its poor then us individual citizens pick up on this vibe and may replicate it in our personal lives.

Vulnerability is the key here. Do you see yourself as vulnerable? Perhaps not. Perhaps you'd rather not think that way and would regard vulnerability as a shameful thing. But then, vulnerability does not necessarily mean hopeless or helpless or inadequate. Children are vulnerable but they are often full of joy. It is often the vulnerability of other people that is the key to loving them.

Knowing our own vulnerability is a step towards having compassion for ourselves. The things that seem to make our lives happy (if indeed we are happy) can sometimes be things that we might easily lose – short-term pleasures and superficial happiness. Compassion for self asks instead about what will make our lives worthwhile in the long-term. What would it mean – towards the end of our lives – for us to say to ourselves that we have lived a good life?

And so too with other people. What are their lives about? What would be a good life for them? This is the kind of big picture that I think it's helpful to consider when faced with some dilemma about what to do amongst family or friends. Can we build other people up? Can we multiply their gifts so they can feel fulfilled in their lives? These are, admittedly, big questions to be asking when our arguments with others are often over very trivial things. And there might be a temptation then to be digging too deep, trying to analyse other folk, and even offering them cures! But no. That's not what I'm suggesting! To offer someone some kind of advice about their life is really an affront. It could easily be even more hurtful than just getting angry!

So the very subtle thing we might think about (and this is why we need to buy time) is to find the right words to build someone up without in any way suggesting how they might change their lives!

Could nations find similar responses? Two principles of government we might consider here are that government is for the protection of a nation's citizens and government is for the flourishing of its citizens. 'Protection' does not have to mean threatening violence against any other nation who we might consider aggressors. In fact, such a stance may make the nation more rather than less vulnerable to attack, and would therefore be a failure of that duty of government to protect its citizens. Protection could instead be by way of shelters, food stocks, emergency power generation, civil defence, cyber defence and back-up means of keeping infrastructure functioning if there were a loss of computer systems.

But the bigger picture here is to consider that second point – human flourishing. The people of other nations need to flourish just as much as our own people. Indeed, so much is now globally connected that we are really talking about all of us flourishing together or all of us failing together.

I won't get into the details of what these

thoughts might lead to by way of policies. But we can certainly think of such things as free trade, free movement of people, immigration, refugees and of course international aid and international diplomacy. Empire is over – unless it is the empire of all humanity, or of the whole Earth biosphere. Today, I think, our level of pride in our nation should be based on its level of compassion. That is my belief. That is my hope.

Another Pudding is Possible

The E Word

In which the author and his Dad visit a local beach and are caught up in a moment of .. of... of...

As I've said, I had returned home to be a carer for my elderly father. We are on the East coast of Scotland, in the county of Fife. My Dad and I would often take a trip down to the south of Fife on a Sunday. Dad was particularly fond of an old hotel in the town of Crail that serves excellent meals. On the way back, we would stop off at the beach near the small town of Kingsbarns. Dad was too frail to go on the beach, but he would sit in a little shelter that is there, looking over the view of the bay, whilst I stretched my legs for a walk. The open rafters of the shelter hosted several swifts' nests.

On one particular visit, baby swifts were just emerging from their nests and getting ready for flight. The parent birds were swooping in and out of the shelter with food for the young fledglings. The swift catches its prey on the wing and spends most of its life airborne. These fledglings, once they took to the wing, would set off soon for Africa, spend our winter there and then head back north, possibly to this same little shelter on the coast of Fife. After my walk along the beach, I sat down beside Dad in the shelter to watch the parent swifts' busy food deliveries and their fledglings precariously perched outside the nests, giving their wings some experimental flaps.

Both father and son have a certain anxiety about life sometimes, although they express it in different ways. These rare moments of calm – looking out over the bay of Kingsbarns, and watching the swifts come and go – are medicine for us both. I think it is my happiest memory of Dad.

That little moment of calm was just a lucky accident, you might say, but it leads me on to thinking about the nature of pleasure.

For many folk it seems that pleasure is the thing they seek in life and possibly pleasure of what might be termed the superficial kind – food, drink, holidays, houses, cars, gadgets, clothes. Someone successful in getting all these things might say that their life is thereby complete – there is no need to do anything else, they have 'arrived'. And who am I to say otherwise?

But others might counter that whilst all of those material things are good to have, it is shared pleasures that are the most important. Hence, intimacy, family and friendship are the true basis of pleasure because nothing that we might own is really any good unless we can share it with others. Well, we might not want to share absolutely everything! But even so, shared pleasure is a helpful notion.

We could go on to say that pleasure is therefore a kind of two-way street. We share gifts of pleasure with others and we receive gifts back in return. It is only true pleasure when it is a gift. I'm a bit more ambivalent about this one! It sounds like sharing has become a rule to which we must abide and that personal, individual pleasure is a bit suspect. But even so, seeing pleasure as a gift is helpful. It is especially helpful, I think, when we consider that our personal happiness is tied up with the society in which we live. The sharing of our gifts then might not be just with people we know or meet but just as much a sharing with society at large.

Many would say that there needs to be a bit of purpose mixed in with our pleasure before we can achieve some kind of lasting happiness or joy. Pleasures come and go, but we can choose to step towards our passion and our enthusiasm and it is this choosing which leads to our flourishing. There's a narrative being created in each person's life and that narrative is, above all, the things we choose in order to bring pleasure into our lives. To be compassionate towards ourselves then is to see our lives with a broader view. What will make us happy in the long-term? Will we be able to look back on our lives from old age and feel that life has been worthwhile? I like this idea of narrative, but then someone who writes is almost bound to say this! There's probably a lot of people who would not consider that they are trying to build a story with their lives.

What we could say at this point is that pleasure is a very personal thing. We all have different pleasures, and to try to grade them in some way

– superficial, profound, low-brow, high-brow – is not that helpful. But let's go back to where we started, with that little moment of calm and contemplation in nature.

Here is where I may lose you, dear reader! Because I'm going to call that time watching the swallows with my Dad an enchantment!

I don't mean, of course, enchantment in the sense that the word is used in a fantasy novel or in mythology.

So what do I mean? I mean enchantment as something that completely captures our attention for a while – makes us stop and look or listen, taste, sniff or touch. Makes us feel that we are briefly outside of ourselves and part of something larger.

I don't mean, necessarily, that enchantment is a spiritual experience. Most, if not all pleasure is rooted in the body. So I'd say you don't need to be a spiritual person to be enchanted. In fact, that's the good thing about enchantment – you don't need to be clever or have 'good taste' or any such thing in order to have an experience of enchantment. So what do you need?

Time, for one thing. Time to be able to stop and look or listen or whatever so that the enchantment can overtake you. And also, something that's more difficult to define. I suppose I'd call it a mind that's open to enchantment. But like I say, that does not mean a clever mind or a superior mind or anything of that sort. Perhaps it is just a mind open to new experiences and able to be astonished and overwhelmed by life.

Enchantment then cannot be put in a bottle and sold to us! But could we at least make it more likely to happen? If we were building a utopia, would we be able to put pleasure and enchantment at its core?

Many stories of utopia start with food, drink, comfortable buildings and perhaps advanced technology. Then, if they are a little more savvy, utopia-builders will recognise our need for good relationships and the link between personal happiness and good governance plus well-functioning societies.

There are some openings for enchantment in all this perhaps, but it is only really when we get to culture that we're anywhere near creating enchantment deliberately.

Human-made things. Literature. Music. Art. Sport. It's difficult to begin describing how any of these can create enchantment. And of course, the enchantment might be there for some and not for others. But even so, I think we should always set our sights on utopia and I think we should always aim for enchantment. Stories, as I've eluded to above, are what make us – we are immersed in story, and story is fantasy as well as enchantment. But we have gone into dangerous territory with the kinds of fantasy we serve up today. Our abiding myths are of eternal progress and conquering heroes – and those heroes make their conquests through power and often violence. And strangely today's fantasies focus on dystopias rather than utopias – utopias are sneered at as silly, despite this belief in eternal progress and technological advancement. So we have to be careful to distinguish between fantasy and enchantment in story. Enchantment is seeing the beauty in the here and now and the familiar rather than trying to conquer and dominate the world. Enchantment can bring a utopia about by seeing the world differently instead of desperately trying to change the world.

We have our model – our examples – in nature. Somehow she can always enchant us, if we let her. So we need to let nature's wildness into our lives, both literally and metaphorically. We need to be wild of body, mind and soul.

And that leads me to the final ingredient for a utopia – to be able to bring people to that state of being that let's us appreciate enchantment when it shows up. We might say that this is part of human flourishing, but again it is very difficult to give expression to exactly what might be involved. All that I can think to say is that some peace, some stillness and some silence is involved.

Enchantment is beauty really – and perhaps you'd have preferred if I'd said beauty all along! But it is more that just the beauty of an object, a place or a person. Enchantment is beauty as a gift of grace.

I wish we could bottle it! I really wish we could. But failing that I hope you'll look out for it and relish it when it arrives. Without enchantment the world is dead.

Another Pudding is Possible

Man on a Bike

Why do some people get better with age whilst others seem to get worse?
It's a tough call, to try to figure this one!

In my home town of Newport, there is a man cycling his way along the road that runs beside the river. His shop is in the town, just beside the main bus stop. Here he gets off and ties up his bike ready for the day's work. No matter the weather, he will greet you and tell you that it's a wonderful day. He always has time for a chat and is always upbeat.

The man lives in a big house and his business is thriving, so you might conclude that the man on the bicycle has good reason to be optimistic about life. However, it was not always so. Forty years previous and that same man – or so it seems to me – had a completely different character. I might have just been blind to his true nature, but back then it would have appeared highly unlikely that he would become the relaxed, friendly and positive person that he subsequently became. What happened to allow this to be?

Well, despite his business success there had been struggles in the man's life. Perhaps this was part of the story. But I think the seeds of success were always there, despite the ups and downs of life. And wisdom seems to grow for some folk – they take on a broader perspective, they learn to relax, they learn to let go, they learn to be open and welcoming to other people. Perhaps it's the happiness level that tips us towards this, or some leaning towards optimism, or some combination of all these factors.

Whatever it is, one thing's for sure. If I could ask for anything for myself for the future it would be to gain that kind of quiet and settled soul the man on the bicycle seems to possess.

Some people just seem to change for the better over time! And some people, it has to be said, change for the worse. If we're going to get a handle on what brings about good change then it will help to first take a look at what stops us changing or makes us worse.

Most of us inherit the way we respond to the world through our parents and to some extent via the society into which we are born. That response may – to put it mildly – be a position that lacks trust. The world, we think, is a harsh place so you need to be tough. You need to be on the defensive against people who may screw you over. And the list of who that might be can include family, teachers, bosses, the police, the government, big business, other nationalities, other genders – in fact, just about anyone. So such a person starts to form a shell around them to protect them from the world, and as they get older the shell just gets harder. Fear therefore could be said to be the root cause of all this, but it might as easily be grief for the kind of family and home they have never had in their lives or have somehow lost. Or it may be despair over the circumstances in which they grew up and which are now repeating in their lives. The fear, grief or despair may express itself as anger.

So how instead might things go well, or how might they be put back on track? Well, as we said with the man on the bicycle, someone might just be lucky and be born into good circumstances. Or they may inherit a very positive personality, such that no amount of trouble can put them down. But for most of us, if we have trouble from our past, any breakthrough can take decades. The problem is that we don't decide for ourselves the kind of outlook we have on life – we just grow into it. As such, it is so much part of ourselves that we are not aware that there are any alternatives. Anyone suggesting alternatives to us is likely to be treated with anger and suspicion, because our protective shell wants to keep out thoughts about things being different. Such a thought would be too frightening.

All this is not to say that such people – I mean people who might struggle to change – are bad people. This is not a matter of goodness and badness. It's about how we view the world. And if we view the world as threatening then inevitably we will be defensive and possibly depressed and angry into the bargain.

But we could certainly say that if these problems could be overcome then we'd have better people and happier people. So how is it done?

The problem is that for most of us, a lot of the

time, our true feelings are hidden from ourselves. So the process must be to identify in ourselves all those things that we fear or that make us grieve or that depress us or make us angry. If possible, we have to start very young. If parents have failed, or if a child has no parents then it is in the education systems that the work must be done. We need to teach compassion for self and compassion for self starts with recognising and trying to understand what's going on inside our heads. And then it's about finding self-worth and knowing that we can grow up having some control over our lives. And finally it's to know that we have specific gifts within our characters and we can use those gifts to serve our family and friends and the wider community.

Well, you may be thinking, the school system is already stretched to breaking point! It doesn't have time for all this touchy-feely stuff! But I urge you to consider that producing pupils who are emotionally aware and have got some way towards knowing who they are, may, in the long-term, be a lot more valuable than just trying to get kids to pass exams. Someone who has got it together as a person will choose to learn and develop their skills. Someone who hasn't got it together will not flourish, no matter how much knowledge you try to cram into them.

Utopian? Yes, it certainly is utopian! Let's take a moment to consider some of the features of utopias so we can see where this compassion for self fits in.

An abundance of stuff is the first rung on the utopian ladder. Food, clothes, amazing houses and public buildings, incredible technology. Some utopian writers (usually male) think that if we could only provide ourselves with this type of cornucopian abundance then everything else would sort itself out.

We can probably appreciate that just providing people with sufficient goods and services is never going to be enough. So the next rung on the utopian ladder is some kind of governance system so things can be properly organised.

Then I'd add a third thing. We need some kind of wow-factor – what I'd like to call enchantment. Nature is always able to provide this, but nature is being systematically destroyed right now. We need to bring her back so she can carry on that work of enchantment. We need to re-enchant. And so too with the human environments that we build, the clothes we wear, the work we do, the tools we use, the food we eat. Having sufficiency of all those things would be good, yes, but that is not a utopia. Instead we need to know our pleasures and create enchantment in all that we do.

This is where we have our first glimpse of the notion that people need to change a bit before we can see the works of our imagination and creativity realised in the world. For it's one thing (and difficult enough) to create enchantment. It's quite another for people to be open to receiving it. That might sound elitist, and I certainly don't intend it to be, because I think there is sufficient range of pleasures and enchantments – wow-factors – to suit all tastes and all types of people. It is the enchantment that the man on the bike is able to receive that makes the <u>real</u> difference in his life! And I know this sounds obscure – I know there may be more obvious ways to improve peoples' lives and to make society safer, happier and more prosperous. But I think this ability to be open to enchantment is the real key! We need to slow down and really know our pleasures – and that's a lot more difficult than it sounds. But I hope the benefits are obvious.

Finally then, a fourth utopian ingredient – the subject of this piece of writing – and what we might call compassion for self. Again, the need for people to change, and unfortunately for would-be utopians, a very difficult work. But yes, compassion for self is part of the care that undergirds all societies and needs to be brought to the fore, as a major ingredient in how society works. We need to raise people with a bit of self-awareness, a bit of wisdom, a bit of soul.

You may feel this is all too much to ask. But I point out that most societies try to do many of the things I've mentioned in one way or another. It's not want of trying that's the problem, it's lack of a joined-up vision. So let's not give up. Let's dare to dream big! Let's aim for utopia!

Take That Lady to Bingo!

A Glasgow woman just wanting to go to bingo sparks a whole debate about local and national politics!

I had travelled with a group of friends to the small town of Falkland in Fife, Scotland for a green festival called 'The Big Tent'. A few of us had been involved with trying to establish a Transition Town group in Dundee, and we were keen to attend a talk about the Transition Movement, scheduled for the afternoon.

There are hundreds of people at the festival, but when we reach the venue for the Transition talk, there's only a few of us. The host looks a bit deflated. Even so, she gets going with her presentation. After a few minutes, she mentions a project in Glasgow that had intended to set up a community garden scheme. This is not a Transition project as such, but one of the audience suggests it might be worth discussing.

So we chat about this. The land in question lies to the rear of houses. It is frequented by drug addicts. The project leaders, we are told, did their best to spark enthusiasm in the locals to establish vegetable gardens and orchards. Apart from the general lack of interest in food growing, the main concern is that increased access to the land may, in turn, increase the incidence of drug use, and may also encourage vandalism.

In desperation, our host had asked one resident what she really wanted. What would make life better for her? The elderly resident said she was frightened to go out alone. She really wanted to go to play bingo, if she could find someone willing to go with her.

There is silence in the venue at this point. The statement hung in the air. I don't remember if anyone actually said it, but we were all thinking – why not ditch the community garden and take that lady to bingo!

So there's the problem right there, for people who might wish to make the world a better place! What do you do if people just don't want the changes you're proposing? What do you do if people actually want something that's harmful for them or for their neighbours or for nature or the planet? (Not that bingo is in this category of course! But what if the lady had wanted to go big-game hunting!)

Real politics is about what happens in your street and in your neighbourhood. And I'm very much a fan of this style of politics – it's come to be known as deliberative democracy. Everyone has a voice in deliberative democracy and your street could be getting together to talk about stuff that could be done right now to make life a bit better. So it might be gardens, fences, litter collection, traffic calming measures, street lighting. At a slightly bigger scale, it might be the local park, play areas, shops and small businesses.

You may like the sound of that. Or you might prefer it if all this were left to big government to organise for us. The 'bottom-up' method (that is, the deliberative democracy I've been describing) is possibly going to deliver the goods more effectively. But then, it takes participation by at least some of the neighbourhood to actually make it happen. And participation might not be your thing. Or it might not be something that anyone in the neighbourhood wants.

But if it did happen, this deliberative thing, then we are back to that problem with which we started. What about that person who just doesn't agree? Or a group of people who disagree? Or several groups just wanting different things? It's not going to be a fun way of spending an evening!

That's why most of us, if we think about such matters at all, would prefer to leave it to those who are paid to take care of this stuff. The top-down method of organising things might be a blunt instrument – no matter how much money is thrown at it – but at least some of the time it gets the job done. And if people don't like what's done for them they can always complain to the government. It doesn't have to end up with a fight between neighbours.

But big government has it's own problems. And the bigger it gets – that is, the closer we get to the top – then the worse the problems seem to be. Governments are complex beasts of course, but we could summarise it's problems with just one word – equity. Or we might simply say, fairness. Because whatever the issue, someone, somewhere will say that they have been treated unfairly. So to solve things is to try to work out what is fair for everyone involved (and we might include other nations, nature and the planet into that fairness equation as well).

But we could dig a bit deeper and say that the real underlying fairness is that (more than likely, depending on what country you're in) we never get to choose what type of government we have in the first place. Sure, we can vote, support one party or another, and maybe get our voices heard a little via a representative democracy. But we never got to choose whether to have a representative democracy in the first place and we're very unlikely ever to get a say in having a different system. Constitutional change is just not on the agenda. Maybe that doesn't bother you. Maybe you don't think that's unfair. Or maybe you'll tell me to go live somewhere else! But where else?

So if we compare those two systems, deliberative democracy and representative democracy, then you'll see that the issue with deliberative democracy is sorting out the small unfairnesses and the issue with representative democracy is that we get stuck with some very big unfairnesses and can't do much about them. In fact the two systems – although they are at opposite poles in terms of bottom-up versus top-down – nonetheless both have kind of a hierarchy arrangement. There has to be representation from the street level in deliberative democracy out to the wider circles of government. And as we work our way out from neighbourhood to town to county, the two systems become more similar. The key thing though is participation – that's what deliberative democracy offers that is mostly lacking in representative democracy.

To change between the two systems does not require a revolution. It could be a gradual shift – that's if we were ever to want the change. Because, whilst we might grumble about unfairnesses, both small and large, we're often not willing to participate in order to set them right. Perhaps (apart from disagreeing with neighbours) the problem is that we don't really believe that our voice could be heard, because we've grown so used to big government ignoring us? Perhaps we think that if we were to raise some substantial issue – let's say a national issue – at a neighbourhood meeting, it just could not work its way up the hierarchy from neighbourhood to town to county to region to nation – finally reaching the level where it could be addressed. The one thing worse than people not having a voice at all is to offer us a voice and then fail to hear. So the system needs to be very very good to fulfil its promise and perhaps that just seems too big an ask – it's participatory utopia.

Well, trouble is it's likely most of us have grown up never discussing issues with neighbours. Unless we happen to live in a co-housing or an eco-village project, we have zero skills in the art of community. There's one key ingredient that's needed – trust. And that takes us right back to the woman and her bingo. Because if we look at it again we might see that it's not an all or nothing thing. There never needs to be a 'crunch' decision, a unanimous agreement, or total success versus total failure. Street politics is a conversation, and it's always changing and evolving. So I think we should take the political problems on the chin and get involved where we can, plus push for the kind of local networks and decision-making processes that could be the basis for a full-scale deliberative democracy. Participation, fairness, trust. They're all important, but maybe it begins with trust.

109

Another Pudding is Possible

Three Bus Trips

In which strange happenings on public transport lead to thoughts about trust and how we might seek to change our neighbourhoods and our nations.

The car had gone. Partly because it needed repairs I could not afford, but also because of my growing dislike for cars generally, and the blight they cause to our towns and cities. I can now look down smugly at drivers, especially those with 4x4's and SUV's!

So, I am waiting on a bus one afternoon with a couple of other folk at the stop. It is just a short hop between towns to visit friends, but then a longer journey to follow later that same day. The bus pulls up at the stop a little late. The door opens but the driver puts up his hand to hold us back from boarding. There is a drunk man on the bus harassing the driver. The driver

111

phones the police. He gets out of the bus and the drunk man follows him. He is filming the driver on his mobile phone and challenging him to a fight. The driver, a much larger man, is still on the phone to the police. The police suggest to the driver that he boards us new passengers waiting at the stop, and try to leave the drunk man out on the pavement. The driver manages to communicate this to us in a low voice whilst the drunk man continues his rant. We pick our moment and clamber abroad. The door closes and the bus pulls away with the drunk man left behind, as planned. The wail of a police siren can be heard as we leave the town. When the bus reaches my destination, I congratulate the driver for keeping his cool in such a difficult situation. He is dismissive, but I think he's pleased by the recognition.

Another leg of the journey and there are two drunk men at the bus stop. They are standing almost nose to nose, muttering a slurred conversation. They begin wheeling around, as if engaged in some strange waltz. It's not clear, but it looks as if one of them may be holding a knife to the other's ribs. There are not many people around and certainly no-one who looks capable of pulling apart two drunk men, if things get out of hand. It sounds like the two men may be cousins. A sorry tale of family struggle unfolds as they continue to wheel around in their weird dance. A bus arrives and passengers bundle abroad with a collective sigh of relief. The drunks aren't getting on the bus.

I think about getting another car.

Now it's the last leg of my journey, and I'm at Dundee bus station. It's not especially late, but it's very quiet. There are only two others there, apart from myself. One is a young woman. She is wearing a short padded jacket and grey leggings. It looks like she is wrapped in a little duvet and her legs are dangling out from underneath. There is also a young man in an enormous padded jacket. He is looking at the electronic displays at each bus stance that provide travel information. He reads them out loud, then circles away to another stance. Then he circles back again and repeats the process. He sees the young woman and walks around in a small circle before heading away to read another display of travel information.

A bus arrives and we all get on. The young woman sits just a couple of seats back from me. The young man is just across the aisle from my own seat. There are only a few others on board and they are elderly and asleep. The young man asks the young woman her name. She responds. There follows an awkward exchange of information on age, place of birth, destination, favourite colour, etc., etc. The young man gets up to sit next to the young woman. He explains that he is on the Autism spectrum and so his behaviour can be erratic. The young woman explains that her brother is in similar circumstances and she is his carer. She has left him with her father for the day, so that she can have some time to herself. Stories of care from relatives and friends now flow both ways. I risk a glance back at the two of them. Their padded jackets are pressed close together like bandages around weary souls.

When I reach home I weigh up these incidents. Two drunken fights versus two stories of care and compassion. Which is the true story of where we are as a society? Or are these all stories of people just trying to make sense of a crazy world?

It's in the streets and amongst cars and buses and shops that we see how society is really working – or not working. Are we frightened even to set foot outside our front doors? Or do we feel safe wherever we go, knowing that people will help if there is a problem? How much do we trust other people? How much do other people trust us? Do we think the government, the police or the health service will look after us? All this is the reality of a society – the human-scale street politics rather than the rhetoric of politicians and business leaders.

I'm not old or frail or otherwise impaired myself, but even so I don't always feel safe on the streets. Think what it's like for the old or for children or young women. And even looking out my window to the street beyond, I see people shuffling by who look like they're only just coping – like the walk to the local shop is about as much as they can manage – and they are only just managing that.

So for me this is where politics should begin. How do we look after those folk who are struggling? How do we keep our children safe? How can we make it safe for a woman to walk home alone at night? Small-scale is, I think, where we can really make a difference – with systems known as cellular democracy or deliberative democracy. Groups of neighbours meet up and discuss how their streets can be safer, cleaner, greener, less threatening, more welcoming. It starts with trust. We have to trust that our neighbours probably have similar needs and concerns as us. We have to trust that even although we don't always agree, yet we are still more or less on the same page. We have to trust everyone will have a voice. We have to trust that things will change because of our efforts!

Because, yes, there is always a temptation to think that it's not worth trying – that nothing will ever change. And then of course there's another leap of faith needed when we scale up to the neighbourhood, the town, the county. Some things just can't get done at street level. And the efforts of the street can simply be squashed by the existing offices of government, unless that simple street politics – the bottom-up politics – can somehow be broadened out. Challenging, for sure!

What do we do then, if we feel it's just us? If we feel that no-one in our street or neighbourhood is ever going to even put their garbage out on the correct day (or even get their garbage to a bin!) let alone organise anything more ambitious?

Well, start where we're at! Be the one who starts something (and always in a polite, gentle, kind, friendly, welcoming way). Don't worry if people say you're naïve or a do-gooder. Just get on and do! Start with positive stuff, not with gripes about how bad everything is.

In the meantime – given that it's unlikely for any of us that constitutional change will take place to bring about a complete system of deliberative democracy – we can nonetheless call out those who hold office within the current system.

Whatever the system, there is someone who is responsible for whatever issue we may have. Start with whoever is immediately responsible, then, if necessary, work up to higher levels of authority. Letters and emails are, I've found, the best way, and it means you can keep a record of correspondence.

Remember these are just people mostly trying

hard to do their job well (and probably struggling). So once again – be polite, gentle, kind, friendly and welcoming! That way (even if you have strong disagreements with their politics) you are nonetheless respecting the offices of government and respecting the humanity of the person you're writing to.

I recognise this will often seem like not enough. Even when we get some responses to our efforts they can seem like we are being politely brushed aside. Or it may be that no-one who we approach actually has the power to change the thing we're concerned about. It would have to be the president or the prime-minister!

Of course there are campaigning groups for a great many of the issues that affect us. Such groups can often have more influence than individuals as they have a stronger voice and greater access to authority.

And then we cross a threshold into protest groups, or what might be called 'activism'. You could say that all that I've mentioned in the preceding paragraphs is activism, but I've a particular meaning for the word that I'd like to pick out.

What we're looking for, I think, is stories about how we'd like the world to be. We started by thinking on the street-level and had a story about streets safe for children, where neighbours will look out for each other and where people will feel safe and welcomed. We could expand that out to how we'd like our neighbourhood to feel. Or our town, our county or our nation or the planet. It's all stories – narratives of how we'd like our world to be.

So my definition of activism is simply this – start living the narrative that you believe in. As Ghandi said, be the change you'd like to see in the world.

Some of that 'being the change' will mostly be hidden – just stuff that's in our own personal life. But don't worry if that goes unseen, because it makes a difference nonetheless. You're living your message and that affects everything you do and say. In fact, this is the bedrock, because unless we are genuinely grounded in our values then any campaigning or protest or politics we might choose to do will not be authentic. And people have a very keen eye for hypocrisy!

Remember context! Meet-ups with family and friends are not opportunities to beat them over the head with your latest political theory! Likewise, any activities at street level are at the most about a vision for the street, not a vision for world government!

Finally, with some trepidation, I mention the kind of campaigning that spills over into violent or illegal protest.

Firstly (assuming you are reading this in the US, the UK, or another Western democracy) we are very lucky to live in a nation that honours free speech and freedom of the press. But there are lines drawn, so to speak, by all nations and it's correct, I think, that there are lines. We might mention peaceful protest – demonstrations, marches, rallies – which, though they may be disruptive, are nonetheless not breaking any laws. The lines are wavering a bit here in the UK at the moment as a result of disruption to road traffic and other transport links – mainly by various climate protest groups. We hope very much that these peaceful demonstrations will still be seen as legal. But there can be protests that really do break the law and there can be angry exchanges online. Where does that cross the line, to become abuse, violence, hate speech or incitement to riot?

Why, I often wonder, do people feel the need to resort to such extremes? Some might conclude that there are just bad people out there. But my conclusion is that (whilst there are a few genuinely bad folks) a lot of people feel they have no voice and they're angry no-one will listen. So violence is a way to be heard. But no, it's a mistake. Violence begets violence. Even if it's a revolution you want then it has to start with the values you think should hold after the revolution has been achieved! And that's not likely to include hate speech and violent insurrection! So we are instead back to stories and remember the famous slogan – if you can't dance then it's not my revolution!

You've probably guessed that I'm on the peaceful protest side of things and think that anger and threats of violence will actually diminish whatever cause people may be trying to promote.

So, yes, if we're thinking of the big stuff we should be thinking of joy, celebration, creativity, enchantment, the sensuous, the profound, the hilarious, the places of abundant generosity, friendship and intimacy. If then, we feel the need to protest, the way we can go about it is in the spirit of these values.

Rope Story

In which a late night visitor leads to adventures in socially-engaged art.

It's late on a Friday evening and I am lying exhausted on the sofa. Rain is falling heavily outside the window. Dad is at his desk, working on his stamp collection.

The doorbell rings. I am off the sofa and away to the front door in an instant. It's very unusual for us to have visitors unannounced. At the door is a friend of mine, Kimberley. She has a bicycle loaded with bags and is soaked to the skin. Hardly before we can speak, Dad has appeared behind me in the doorway. He seems terrified, and staggers back into the house. Since Dad has met Kimberley on a few occasions before, this is a bit puzzling, but perhaps he has not recognised her, or it is just the surprise of someone showing up late at night.

119

I usher Kimberley into the house and we unload her bike and put stuff out to dry on radiators. Then I set about making some food. Meanwhile, Dad has barricaded himself into his bedroom. Despite the lure of wine and extra biscuits, I cannot tempt him out to join us. Then the sofa is folded down for Kimberley and I see Dad into his own bed. He still wants his door closed, so I leave mine open so I can hear him if he needs help during the night.

The next day, Saturday, I suggest to Kimberley we head into Dundee, where an arts group have organised an event. I leave breakfast out for Dad, who still refuses to leave his room until Kimberley has gone. Then I leave a lunch for him in the fridge and set off to cycle with Kimberley into Dundee. Luckily the rain has stopped.

The event the artists have organised involves carrying a large length of rope through the streets of Dundee. We start off at a jute museum and then meander through the city, stopping at a few venues along the way.

The third stop is outside one of Dundee's theatres. Here, we set the rope down and split up into pairs. One out of each pair is blindfolded and must be led by the other across the rather complicated front entrance grounds of the theatre. I am one who is blindfolded. It is something of a perilous trip. For genuinely blind people, I can imagine their guide dogs tendering their resignations. But with careful guidance, the journey is completed. Then we pick up the rope again and carry on our way.

After a few more stops, we arrive at last beside the River Tay. The tide is out and there are mud-flats stretching out from the shoreline. One of the artists, who is working on projects related to water, climbs down the stone steps to try to collect some of the river water in a test tube. When she steps off the last step, onto the mud, she immediately sinks to her knees. She is only a short woman, so there isn't much left of her before things could get tricky. We are all immediately alert, and I think that perhaps the rope is about to find a very practical use! Luckily though, a sample of water is collected and the woman returns safely up the steps. The water in the test tube is filthy.

We settle again and at this point two children are approaching, heading for the nearby swimming pool. The leader of the artists' group speaks to them. They tell him that they come from one of the housing estates in the suburbs of Dundee. They say that they feel safe coming into the centre of town together, but there are other parts of the city where they do not feel safe. It strikes me as remarkable that such frank answers to these questions should have been given to a strange group of people sitting with a coil of rope.

What was the rope walk really about, you may be wondering? Well, like many artworks, it leaves us open to bring our own interpretations, and sometimes these can add to or diverge from the original intent of the artist. Some might not like this prospect, but for others part of the gift of art is that it invites new ideas and new imaginings as it goes along. For what it is worth then, here's my interpretation.

As perhaps you'll be aware, Dundee was once famous for its manufacturing industry based around jute. So we started off in a jute museum, which had, in fact, once been a jute mill. The journey through the town was, if you like, the unravelling of the material economy of jute, back to its original source – the river that brought the boats in with the raw materials from Asia, and of course, also back to its original source in nature herself. On the way, whilst Dundee's material economy unwinds, its cultural economy winds up. We stop off at university buildings, theatres, an arts centre and a science centre. And then our main stop, with the blindfolds. There is a side to our economies that remains hidden – and as such, we are blind to it – and this is care. All of our economies are supported by this, but it is, in turn, unacknowledged. We might even look at where we stopped for our blindfolded walk. Perhaps it tells us that the way to bring to society's attention its reliance on care is through narrative – through stories. So the theatre, and the arts generally, are a potential source.

What made the whole of the event so memorable for me was that it was sandwiched between two examples of fear – my Dad's fear of a stranger arriving late at night and the children's fear about going into certain parts of the city. Both relate back to care. If you are a carer you will know that we can only do our best. An old person often has irrational fears that we might try to assuage, but might fail to completely calm. For children, perhaps there is more we can achieve. What better way for us to think about our towns and cities than to see them as places where children need to feel safe. And if we prepare them properly for life then they will grow in courage and strength into adulthood and then take on those responsibilities of care themselves.

Kimberley set off to visit other friends after the rope day and I went home to get Dad his dinner. After a few days more, he said to me one evening, 'Kimberley's really quite a nice girl, isn't she?'

The rope story is an example of a 'socially engaged' artform. Typical of its genre, it sought to raise issues but not prescribe solutions. Those artists might say that, like much art, a playful exploration of its subject invites us to dance our own solutions. If we think carefully about the story it includes five different types of economy – the material, the cultural, the spatial (the place of Dundee), the natural and the emotional (through care). There were references to the circular nature of all economies and a little of how the economies keep going through gift – especially as explored through care – the emotional economy. Also, of course, a strong link to a particular place and to nature. When we say the word 'economy' then, we need to spare a thought for what it is we are really talking about. Only once we take on a much broader view will we really get an economy that works for everyone and for nature.

In the meantime, all we can do is keep caring.

Acknowledgements

The move back home to care for my father was strangely blessed by a whole set of new people who arrived into my life at that time. The group of artists originally met as Dundee Artists in Residence (D-AiR). Some of the artists who were part of D-AiR also went on to be part of the Dundee Commons group – 'If the city were a commons'. Special thanks to Jonathan Baxter, Sarah Gittins, Joanna Foster and all other members of these groups, and to Kimberley Ellis.
Information on the commons project can be found here:
https://onsiteprojects.wordpress.com/if-the-city-were-a-commons/

Printed in Great Britain
by Amazon